# The Power of Unconditional Self-Love

Danny Skyfeather

# Contents

*This book is dedicated to the inner children of divine light and innocence within us all.*

Danny Skyfeather

# Introduction

Hello and welcome. Before we begin, maybe you could give yourself a moment. Take a deep breath, filling and emptying your lungs completely, and *relax*. Take another deep breath. Place a warm hand on your chest and send yourself some much needed care and compassion. Then ask yourself, *Am I willing to love myself on such profound levels as to heal, uplift, and transform every area of my life?* A little willingness is all it takes to begin. Just a little. Take one more deep breath and *imagine* how your life will look and feel when you love yourself with fierce gentleness and loyal tenacity.

Genuine and transformational self-love begins with honoring where you are and where you have been from an honest and compassionate perspective. Do you need to love yourself more? Is negative self-talk or self-hatred an issue for you? If so, please know that there is nothing wrong with you. You're okay. We all have the remnants of past conditioning lingering inside us. All too often, this old stuff comes up at the absolute wrong time to wreck our relationships and wreak havoc on our emotional and physical health.

In these pages you will learn how to access the energy of love and direct it into your cells, body, heart, and mind. By using the intelligent energy of love in this way, you can heal yourself on levels where language and intellect are unable to reach.

You will learn a specific mind/body method of breathing to rapidly absorb the potent affirmations, which I call "heart-commands," into the deepest levels of your consciousness. This method will access the powers of your mind, emotions, and physiology to swiftly populate your subconscious mind with potent thoughts of unconditional self-love.

In this book, you will also be introduced to the Twelve Steps of Unconditional Self-Love. These steps resemble the traditional 12 steps in some ways. In other ways, they are vastly different. They contain key statements which mark our heart-centered decision to move our minds, bodies, and lives into the light of our own passionate and sincere self-love.

Further, when you diligently and persistently engage the Four Daily Practices of Unconditional Self-Love in this book for 90 days, you will spark an inner transformational process that will continue for your lifetime. By 1) breathing the energy of love, 2) breathing and absorbing the heart-commands, 3) doing mirror work, and 4) practicing self-care... you will be merging into a new and elevated version of yourself. You will be intentionally creating a future that reflects your highest love and respect for yourself.

Self-love improves our health, our sleep, our state of mind and heart, our relationships, and helps improve our spiritual connection with the universe. Every area of our lives will be touched.

This work is not a quick fix and can be challenging at times. The energy of love is intelligent and will cause all sorts of healing and transformation within you. This work will help you tap into and feel elevated emotions like love, joy, gratitude, delight, awe, wonder, and enthusiasm, etc. It will help uplift your relationships to higher levels of clarity and connection. It will help you fall in love with the sheer magic and joy of being alive. It will help you witness how brilliant *you truly are* on so many levels.

My goal in writing this book is to help you raise your consciousness to the highest love that you are – and to love yourself from that elevated perspective. Please also keep in mind that this book is an invisible type of mastermind. As you do this work, you are energetically joined with everyone else doing the same thing. We silently enliven and strengthen each other's practice. For this, please feel my waves of love and gratitude for stepping up and being here.

*Danny Skyfeather*
*April, 2020*

# The Power of Love

In this book, we will be working deeply with the vibrational energy of love in a heightened way to heal and transform our bodies, minds, and lives. Here is a statement that reflects and embodies the joyous power of this love...

~~~

Love is total acceptance. Love meets me where I am and others where they are. Love is ever-deepening compassion toward myself and others in our shared humanity. Love is immovable and unshakeable presence. Love is fearless in its courage to be fully open and vulnerable. In the vulnerability of love the invincibility of my soul is found. Love awakens the genius in myself, my community, and the world.

Love is omniscient, omnipresent, and omnipotent. Love is equally present in all moments and in all places at once, and with the silent power that gives life to everything.

Love is intelligent energy that knows where to go inside me, what to do, and according to perfect and divine timing. Love easily heals bones, bodies, emotional wounds, and relationships. Love patiently outlasts everything that only seems to appear contrary to itself.

Love is a perpetual, beautiful, and inexhaustible river, blessing and freeing the giver as it passes through. Love is the most magnetizing and manifesting force in the universe.

Love awakens perfect health, wholeness, vitality, and vigor – flowing best through the conduit that believes in itself as love. Love embodies total freedom and my highest abundance. Love is perfectly enjoined with gratitude and always flowers open as ecstatic bliss and joy. Love is the very essence of who I am.

~~~

Through the steps, practices, and affirmational heart-commands in this book, the striving aspiration is to perpetually cascade the energy of love through our minds and lives. All our human emotions, experiences, triumphs, setbacks, joys, pains, and pleasures are continuously bathed in this sacred and continuous flow of love.

Unconditional self-love means to develop the inner ability to apply compassion, understanding, and true kindness to ourselves with radical and fierce tenacity. It means to develop *eagle consciousness*, flying forever above our human travels, while showering ourselves with love along the way. It further represents our human courage to accept and receive the love we give ourselves, and to dedicate that love to improving our relationships, communities, and the world.

May our individual self-love join, commingle, and spread inward and onward to serve the collective heart and mind of humanity. This book and all these practices are dedicated to the greater good, beginning with our precious human selves. May self-love heal the world.

# My Journey

I graduated with honors from Self-Hatred University. Even after all these years, the Dean of Admissions of that Institution shows up at my doorstep occasionally and demands that I return to class. Sometimes I do return to class. Most times, however, I refuse. Every day, the flower of my heart opens a little more in the light of my own self-love.

I grew up in the 1970s in Colorado Springs, Colorado. My mom and dad were 33 years apart in age, so their relationship didn't last. Through the experience of emotional, physical, and sexual abuse – I was conditioned early to hate myself. It wasn't a conscious skill, but more like an embedded unconscious program running in the background of my mind all the time.

At the age of six or seven, I smoked pot for the first time. By the age of nine I was a full-blown addict. I diligently practiced my addiction until the age of 19 when I found my way to twelve-step groups. Although I ingested any substance that I could get my hands on, my two main buddies were pot and alcohol.

Pot was my emotional blanket that kept me safe from the raging volcano of emotional pain in my body and mind. Looking back, I am grateful for the substance. Without it, I most certainly would have gone insane. The tragic death of my brother on a motorcycle accident, and the subsequent suicide of my uncle four months later – left my hold on reality in tatters. Staying stoned helped me survive. However, there came a time later in my life where I wasn't using the substance anymore. It was using me. I was a slave to it.

Being high was the normal state of consciousness for me. In high school, I woke up and smoked a bowl of weed before school, then smoked more bowls at lunch, after school, in the evening, and before bed. In all my waking moments, I was either smoking or seeking weed. Being without any substance at all was a living hell.

Alcohol was different. I was in an abusive relationship with alcohol. It was like getting into the boxing ring with an incredibly angry professional boxer. He had no boxing gloves on his fists. Every time I took any amount of alcohol into my system, he would mercilessly lay into me. Blackouts. Violent puking. Hangovers that would last for two days. He beat the living hell out of me every single time I drank. He did so unconditionally. No mercy, ever. The funny thing is that I always went back to him. I was a weekend binge drinker. Going to college in the mountains of Colorado, the alcohol flowed freely and abundantly.

At around age 18, the deep desire to be clean and sober formed in my consciousness. It was like a point of light in the dark haze of blackouts and pot smoke started growing. I dreamed about a sober life, hoped for it, and tried with all my might to quit. One time I decided to camp next to a river and stay there until I had completely cured myself of the desire to ever use or drink again. I had a friend drive me all the way around to the other side of the river where I could access it. I scurried down the steep embankment, confident in my ability to overcome my demons.

Once I was all set up, here come the mosquitos. Nasty little bastards! It was also ridiculously hot. I became agitated, irritated, and uncomfortable. My plan was not working. I think I lasted maybe two hours. I packed up my stuff and had to climb back up the steep ravine to get to the road. It was not easy! Then I walked from 11 pm to 7 am to get back to my dorm.

I tried many other methods and techniques to quit, but none of them worked. Finally, a counselor suggested that I attend twelve step groups. I found the courage and went. In these meetings I encountered the energy of unconditional love for the first time. I was attracted to this energy like a moth to flame. After two short relapses, I put my head down and focused only on meetings and my college courses. I stayed sober and have been free from substances for 33 years.

For the first four years of being sober, I had a big smile on my face that covered up the broiling pain I held inside. After a brief but beautiful romance that ended as quickly as it began, all my pain came gushing out. It was like I cried continuously for two straight years. I was depressed and suicidal, and simply going to meetings and repeating program talk wasn't working.

I sought help, and for the first time in my life I was able to tap into the deeper layer of pain, process it, and get to the other side. The only relief was found in feeling the pain. Nothing else worked.

After about 12 years of being sober, I got married. It was during the early years of this relationship that my conditioned patterns of self-hatred came flooding out. I couldn't handle being on the emotional hot seat. Every time I felt cornered or misunderstood, I would lash out, or become cold and distant.

I remember one incident where we were having an argument. We were in the car, and it was a cold winter night. I reached that point of not being able to handle it anymore. I yelled, got out of the car, slammed it very hard, and stormed away. I had no coat on, so I just walked around the parking lot for 20 minutes in the freezing cold. A day or so later, in reflecting on that fight, I realized (step one) that self-hatred was a major problem for me and that I really needed to start loving myself.

One day, sitting in the sauna at the gym, I just put a hand on my heart and said "I love you." It was the first tiny baby step of self-love. I think it lasted like a day or two, and then I quit. My experience is that in the beginning, when introducing the energy of self-love to a body and mind conditioned over many years to be in a state of toxic shame and self-loathing, that energy feels like poison. It was very hard and painful to love myself in the beginning. Even today, it can still be hard.

I was married for 14 years, and today still count her as my friend. We went through an awful lot together, with painful and joyous moments, and had lots of laughs. She had two children when we met, a young boy with severe autism, and his sister with borderline autism. I immediately immersed myself in them. Raising this beautiful boy, even with all the challenges, was the most important spiritual and emotional discipline of my life. He was and still is today at the age of 25, my soul friend and teacher. His older sister is 28 years old and is the sweetest soul and dearest friend of my heart.

We also adopted three more children from three different continents – and went through a very intense version of parenting hell for five years. At one point I really believed that the stress was going to kill me. We made it through all that and later got divorced. The process of uncoupling was very friendly – and we are still co-parenting our last child. Sometimes marriages need to be upgraded to friendships.

I have been through the trenches and pain of self-hatred. In college I would punch myself in the face in the middle of the night. When I was emotionally upset, I would lay in bed and internally scream thoughts of self-hatred at myself. I blasted them within. I imagined knives cutting my body to pieces. Then I would sob and cry, and then have that self-hatred hangover all the next day.

In the last 30 years I have studied and practiced meditation in several different traditions. I am a certified hypnotherapist. I have studied and practiced Reiki and energy healing modalities. I have raised special needs children. In my day job, I have practiced law as a criminal and family law attorney.

Throughout all of that, I have learned how conditioned self-hatred negatively impacts relationships, increases the struggles of parenting, creates legal challenges, creates dis-ease in the body and emotions, and lowers the quality of life. I have also come to an understanding that the only real solution is doing the transformational work of unconditionally loving ourselves on a deep and energetic level.

This book slowly emerged over the last six years from doing intense healing work and muddling through the depths of emotional pain. It started with the affirmations and the audio recordings. Over that time, I would come back occasionally and re-read and re-listen. This had the effect of watering the seeds that would grow into these pages.

I am so grateful for the traditional 12 steps of recovery as they are written. They served their purpose for me for many years. I came to a point, however, where I had to reach beyond them and get outside help to keep from killing myself. Also, I have never really resonated with all of them. This may be seen as blasphemy by some people "in the rooms" but it represents my experience, nonetheless.

What I tried to accomplish in writing the Twelve Steps of Unconditional Self-Love is to capture what I love about the traditional steps, and to completely abandon the rest. I wrote them to represent a framework and internal process of learning to love myself unconditionally. I share them with you with an open heart.

I don't pretend to be someone who has mastered the art and practice of self-love. However, I do consider myself a perpetual student. There have been many times where I started out strong in loving myself, then hit walls of emotional pain and stopped for months or even years. Sometimes I got knocked off the self-love train. Other times I jumped off. Throughout it all, I always came back again.

This is my message to you: Never stop coming back to loving your sweet and beautiful self. Keep getting up and coming back again no matter what.

Danny Skyfeather

# The Twelve Steps of Unconditional Self-Love

Danny Skyfeather

The following Twelve Steps of Unconditional Self-Love are written from an "I am" affirmational perspective because it is our one-hundred-percent individual responsibility to love ourselves. Nobody else can do it for us. Only we can.

Having said that, we can greatly benefit from the loving presence and support of others in our own process, and we can also benefit from being present with others in their process. We do the work ourselves but not by ourselves. We are together on an energetic level as we do this work.

The steps are commingled and connected with each other. They are not meant to signify a straight line. They represent more of a circular pattern or swirling spiral of growth. For instance, steps one, two, and three circle around and connect with each other. This is because doing this type of work can bring stuff up, and there may be starts and stops along the way. We peel back a layer of the onion and get knocked down, process the experience, then start back again at step one.

Step one is just a realization that we need to love ourselves. Step two is the hope that it will work. Step three is the beginning, the restart, or making a commitment to deepen and strengthen the practice.

Step four is simply writing our history from the vantage point of the future, and with a clear willingness to love and support all earlier versions of ourselves. We can also write a step four on specific periods of our lives, like a relationship that ended or a phase that we have passed through, etc.

Steps six, seven, eight, nine, ten, and eleven can all be completed while writing about our past in step four and in sharing that with someone during step five. As we share our past with someone we love and trust, we come to a deeper awareness of ourselves, make decisions to practice radical self-acceptance and self-love, and realize how our conditioned self-hatred impacted our lives and relationships. We also gain insights into how we can heal and mend that damage, starting with healing our relationship with ourselves.

When it comes time to doing step five with someone, choose someone that you love and trust. You can choose a priest, a friend, or a counselor. You can also go through all the steps by yourself except step five, and then do that one when you feel ready. It is more important to share it with the right person rather than choosing someone you think you "should" do it with. Trust your heart and gut more than your brain.

When you are on the receiving end of step five and have agreed to step into the role of a sacred listener, get prepared internally. Put your own process out of your mind. This is all about the other person. As they share their story, listen with your eyes, your heart, and your body. Be fully present with them. Encourage them to dig deeper for the insights and nudge them along in totally and unconditionally loving the earlier versions of themselves. This is all about them loving themselves. If it feels right to you and them, go through steps six through eleven with them. Repeat the core statements together. This can deepen your process and theirs.

For now, you can read through the twelve steps as you breathe deeply and hold an open hand on the center of your chest. Point them within. This will help to start putting them into your mind and body. You can't go through them too many times. In fact, it is encouraged to come back to them often and repeat the pertinent statements of self-loved contained there. As you read, intend and feel that you are planting the twelve steps as a whole into your mind and body.

The idea is to take these steps from being concepts that you read with your *thinking brain* to being truths that you feel with your *feeling heart*. Ultimately, the goal is to reach a state of heart-brain alignment in absorbing them into your body and mind. The heart-center helps the mind think better. At the same time, the mind can also help the heart-center open and feel on deeper levels. They are meant to work together, and the breath is the thread that connects them both.

Most of all, these steps are written to help us develop a consciousness of loving ourselves unconditionally and from a higher perspective, all while being gentle with ourselves along the way.

Danny Skyfeather

The principles and concepts that are conveyed through these Twelves Steps of Unconditional Self-Love are:

Insight,
Willingness,
Hope,
Decision,
Commitment,
Action,
Courage,
Vulnerability,
Trust,
Self-Awareness,
Self-Acceptance,
Self-Forgiveness,
Self-Responsibility,
Self-Image,
Self-Gentleness,
Self-Understanding,
Tenacity,
Persistence,
Elevated Emotions,
Service, and
Presence.

In later chapters, you will learn The Mind-Chest Tapping Protocol. Feel free to incorporate this method into your practice of working with these 12 steps.

# The Twelve Steps of Unconditional Self-Love

Step 1: I understand that the root cause of much of my suffering is a lack of self-love – and I realize that I need to begin loving myself.

Step 2: I believe that unconditionally loving myself will heal and transform my life.

Step 3: I now begin, continue, and deepen the sincere practice of energetic and unconditional self-love on a daily and persistent basis.

Step 4: I courageously write down where I have been in my life with the willingness to support, embrace, and love all earlier versions of myself.

Step 5: I tap into my vulnerability and share my story with another human being that I love and trust.

Step 6: I look honestly at my conditioned patterns from the deeper understanding that there is nothing wrong with me.

Step 7: I practice radical self-acceptance and self-forgiveness on the deepest levels of my body and mind.

Step 8: I come to understand how self-hatred has hurt myself, other human beings, and my relationships with them.

Step 9: I heal the damage that self-hatred has caused myself and others by building and strengthening a self-image of love toward myself.

Step 10: I practice self-awareness and self-honesty on a daily basis. When I step out of alignment with self-love, I gently guide myself back.

Step 11: Every day I reach for higher perspectives of inner growth. I enjoy ever-upward cycles of expansion that never end. I practice cultivating elevated emotional states of love, joy, awe, wonder, enthusiasm, gratitude, freedom, peace, and delight.

Step 12: I am committed to being present to support others in their process of unconditional self-love. As I hold space for others in loving themselves, I am loving myself on deeper and more fulfilling levels.

*notes:*

Danny Skyfeather

## Step 1:

## I understand that the root cause of much of my suffering is a lack of self-love – and I realize that I need to begin loving myself.

The simple awareness, recognition, and understanding that self-hatred is an issue for me is itself an act of self-love. Even if I am not yet able to begin loving myself, just being present with the truth that I need to love myself is enough to begin. I am okay. Even though I learned to hate myself, this doesn't mean that I will be forever enslaved to self-hatred. What has been learned can be unlearned. What has been conditioned can be reconditioned.

I ask myself: Is self-hatred an issue for me? Is it causing problems and dramas in my relationships? Is it increasing my addictive behavior? Am I noticing self-hatred and shame-based inner talk?

Even if I have been doing this work for many years, I still ask these questions. This is an ongoing process. Again, there is nothing at all wrong with me. I am okay. I am learning to unlearn my patterns of self-hatred, and I am grateful for that.

## Step 2:
## I believe that unconditionally loving myself will heal and transform my life.

I choose to believe that the practice of energetically and unconditionally loving myself will heal and transform my life from within. I cultivate the feeling and awareness of hope. If other people have transformed their lives and relationships through the daily practice of sincere self-love, then I can too.

As I transform the inner landscape of my thoughts and feelings to reflect the highest love for myself, then the outer conditions of my life will change for the better. I am willing to do this work. Even if my first steps are small but steady, I am willing to take them. I believe in the power of self-love.

## Step 3:

## I now begin, continue, and deepen the sincere practice of energetic and unconditional self-love on a daily and persistent basis.

Beginning to love myself unconditionally is as simple as saying *I love you* to myself with sincere feeling and intensity. I now place my hand upon my chest, take several deep, long, inhaling and exhaling breaths – and repeat this statement multiple times with as much feeling as possible:

*I open and expand my chest as wide as possible and say to myself: I love you... I love you... I love you. I point these words into every cell of my body, into every buried emotion within me, and into all the layers of my mind. I love you... I love you... I love you. This simple act is a beautiful beginning and a deepening of this life-long process of self-love that positively transforms my life in every way.*

I decide to continue this process on a persistent basis. I do this through the daily and heart-centered feeling and vibration of potent affirmations, by using my breath and imagination to channel the energy of love through my mind and body every day, and by coming back often to repeat the above statement from within the center of my chest.

I also realize that there will be many times in my journey that I need to begin again, to recommit, and to take my self-love up a notch. There may be many starts, stops, and detours along the way. I am willing to be gentle and kind with myself, and to nurture myself along the way. May I always keep the mind and heart of a beginner.

## Step 4:

## I courageously write down where I have been in my life with the willingness to support, embrace, and love all earlier versions of myself.

The past lives in my cells, my mind, and my memories. By taking the time to thoroughly and courageously write down where I have been, and to do so from the perspective of unconditional self-love, I am energetically and emotionally supporting all earlier versions of myself. Love is the energy and power that transcends all time and space. I am privileged to write my story and use this energy to embrace all moments of my past with compassion, understanding, and acceptance.

All earlier versions of myself are inside me now. They need my love, support, esteem, and encouragement. I honor them by writing down where I have been and by sending my love back in time to support them.

I ask myself: Where have I been? When did I first learn to hate myself? What experiences of abuse or trauma did I have to endure? How did I process that? Writing all this down is enormously healing and powerful. This step can also bring up a lot for me, so I will get support from others as I need it.

Danny Skyfeather

## Step 5:
## I tap into my vulnerability and share my story with another human being that I love and trust.

In my courage to be vulnerable, I find my greatest strength. I choose someone that I love and trust, and I share my story with them. I speak my past aloud to another human being, all while loving and embracing everything that I have been through. There is enormous potential and power in loving myself while in the loving presence of another human being.

## Step 6:
## I look honestly at my conditioned patterns from the deeper understanding that there is nothing wrong with me.

Taking deep inhaling and exhaling breaths, I hold my hand on my heart and repeat this statement multiple times with passion, intensity, and feeling:

*There is absolutely nothing wrong with me. I am a whole, perfect, complete, and precious human being. From this higher perspective, I look honestly at all my conditioned patterns of thought, emotion, and behavior that may not be in alignment with my highest growth. I am grateful to simply become aware of them. Pure awareness is pure love.*

As my journey flows forward, I will come back as often as I choose to repeat and reflect this statement even deeper into my chest, body, and mind.

## Step 7:
## I practice radical self-acceptance and self-forgiveness on the deepest levels of my body and mind.

As I become aware of my conditioned patterns and behaviors in step six, I now make a solemn commitment to practice radical self-acceptance and self-forgiveness. Taking several deep breaths, I place my hand on my heart and repeat this statement multiple times with sincere emotion, feeling, and conviction:

*I radically accept and forgive myself on the deepest levels of my body, mind, and emotions. In all the moments of my life to come, whether an hour from now, a week from now, or even years from now, the powers of self-acceptance and self-forgiveness will continue to grow stronger within me. I radically accept and forgive myself on the deepest levels of my body, mind, and emotions.*

Going forward, I will periodically come back to repeat and reinforce this statement within me as I feel intuitively guided to do so.

## Step 8:
## I come to understand how self-hatred has hurt myself, other human beings, and my relationships with them.

With the powers of self-awareness, self-acceptance, and self-forgiveness growing stronger within me, I survey my past. I look deeper into how the embedded and toxic shame and conditioned self-hatred has hurt me, my health, other human beings, and my relationships with them.

I look at the many ways I have projected my self-hatred onto others. I see the ways in which I relinquished the responsibility to love myself onto others. I see how the false beliefs within me of being unworthy and unlovable have sabotaged my chances and opportunities for love and connection. I look at the fear, shame, and unworthiness within me with clear eyes and an open heart. When I am feeling afraid, ashamed, or unworthy – I bring them into the light of awareness by speaking them aloud.

Taking several deep breaths, I hold my hand upon my chest and repeat this statement multiple times with passionate and emotional intensity:

*Even though shame, feelings of unworthiness, and fear within me has caused harm to myself, other people, and my relationships with them – I love myself anyway. I am still worthy of emotional peace, radiant health, deep connection, and fulfilling relationships. I am lovable in every way. I am committed to becoming more aware of myself from a higher perspective of unconditional self-gentleness and compassion.*

As my life unfolds, I will come back whenever I choose to reinforce this statement within the emotional and energetic layers of my body and mind.

## Step 9:
# I heal the damage that self-hatred has caused myself and others by building and strengthening a self-image of love toward myself.

I heal the damage that self-hatred has caused to myself and others by first and foremost healing the relationship I have with myself. My outer life reflects the inner thoughts, images, feelings, and attitudes that I hold toward myself. It is my sincere, conscious, and deliberate decision to build an internal blueprint and self-image of love toward myself. In this spirit, I place a hand on my chest, take several deep breaths, and state this declaration multiple times with all my heart, soul, and strength:

*As I heal my relationship with myself on the inner levels of my being – my life and relationships will also heal. I choose to cultivate internal mental and emotional images of loving, respecting, caring for, nurturing, and esteeming myself. I see the light in my eyes and the smile on my face. As these images come to me, I activate them inside the energetic and emotional centers of my heart-field. This sincere commitment to build an unshakeable self-image of love toward myself will grow stronger in the days and weeks of my life to come. So it is.*

I will come back to repeat this statement as often as I feel inclined to do so. I can also draw, paint, or color visual scenes and images that represent my new and ongoing self-image of self-love.

## Step 10:
## I practice self-awareness and self-honesty on a daily basis. When I step out of alignment with self-love, I gently guide myself back.

I am grateful to continue my growth on a daily and persistent basis. I realize that this is a long-term process. I am willing to do the work every day. As I practice using my breath and imagination to send the energy of love into and through my cells, heart, and mind every day – I realize that stuff will come up. There will be times that I step out of alignment with self-love. Thoughts and feelings of judgment and hatred may arise toward myself and others. I now take several deep breaths, hold my hand of love upon my chest and repeat this heart-felt decision and commitment multiple times:

*Self-gentleness is self-love. I remind myself of this often as I develop the skills of self-awareness and self-honesty. When I step out of alignment with the principles of love, respect, kindness, and compassion toward myself – I take a step of consciousness above my mind and body. From this higher place, I wrap myself in gentleness and lovingly guide myself back into alignment. I realize that reconditioning my mind and behaviors in self-love takes time, patience, tenacity, and persistence. I am committed to always getting back up and coming back to this sacred practice of unconditional self-love. I never lose the gains I make. They are with me forever.*

As I continue my journey of self-awakening and self-love, I will come back to heart-repeat, feel and reinforce this statement as many times as I need to.

Danny Skyfeather

## Step 11:

**Every day I reach for higher perspectives of inner growth. I enjoy ever-upward cycles of expansion that never end. I practice cultivating elevated emotional states of love, joy, awe, wonder, enthusiasm, gratitude, freedom, peace, and delight.**

I am committed to continuous growth. Every day I reach for higher perspectives, insights, and breakthroughs. As much as it is my responsibility to feel and process emotional pain, grief, sadness, etc., I also get to feel good. I have just as much access to elevated emotional experiences as lower ones. I will try whatever meditations, visualizations, or methods to access them. It is my natural human right to feel good, healthy, alive, vibrant, creative, joyous, abundant, connected, free, and overflowing with positive feelings. I now place my hand upon the center of my chest, take several long deep breaths, and passionately repeat and anchor this statement multiple times from within my chest, cells, mind, and emotions:

*I now call forth the elevated emotional states of love, joy, awe, wonder, enthusiasm, gratitude, freedom, peace, and delight to rise within me. I activate the innate intelligence of my heart-field to bring all these elevated emotions into full feeling and expression. In all the moments of my life to come, whether a day, a week, or even years from now, my heart-field will continue to bring up, manifest, and express feelings of love, joy, awe, wonder, enthusiasm, gratitude, freedom, peace, and delight. This inner process will continue within, below, and beyond my conscious awareness. I give myself permission to feel and experience all elevated emotions.*

I will come back often to deepen and strengthen this statement within my chest, body, and mind on all energetic and emotional levels.

## Step 12:

# I am committed to being present to support others in their process of unconditional self-love. As I hold space for others in loving themselves, I am loving myself on deeper and more fulfilling levels.

We are in this together. As we unconditionally love ourselves in the loving presence of each other, our growth expands. Even though my self-love is my 100 percent responsibility, I am still on this journey with other human beings. In holding the emotional and energetic space for other people to unconditionally love themselves, I am deepening my love for myself. Being present does not mean offering advice, interfering, or overstepping boundaries. Being present means listening and allowing the innate and beautiful self-love in others to grow on its own. My job is to hold the energetic and emotional space for that to happen.

I breathe deeply, place my hand upon my precious heart, and repeat this statement multiple times with passionate and emotional intensity:

*I am committed to being fully present, with an open heart, to support other people in their own process of developing a consciousness of unconditional self-love. I love others as myself and I love myself in others. I am so grateful for the sincere privilege of listening, honoring, supporting, and encouraging my fellow human beings in their process of self-love. So it is.*

I will keep coming back to reinforce this statement from within my emotional and energetic centers. Being present with others is a lifelong skill that I practice with patience, self-care, self-awareness, and self-understanding. I will be loving and gentle with myself along the way.

Danny Skyfeather

# Four Daily Practices of Unconditional Self-Love

# Four Daily Practices of Unconditional Self-Love

There are four daily practices of this process that work in synergistic harmony together:

1. *Breathing the Energy of Love.* This involves a daily session of breathing in a specific way as to channel the energy of love into the deepest levels of your mind and body.

2. *Breathing the Heart-Commands of Unconditional Self-Love.* This involves combining your breath, your heart-center, and your prefrontal cortex to rapidly absorb and assimilate the heart-commands of self-love into your subconscious and unconscious minds.

3. *Unconditional Self-Love Mirror Work.* This involves taking a few moments each day and taking a few deep breaths and channeling the energy of love into your reflection in the mirror.

4. *Self-Care of Body, Mind, and Environment.* This involves taking care of yourself and loving yourself through what you eat, by moving your body, and by caring for your environment.

These four practices can be enhanced by the further daily practices of 5) hand-writing the core heart-command, 6) writing a gratitude list, and by 7) consciously engaging in positive mental and emotional self-talk. You can also incorporate Mind-Chest Tapping into these practices as well.

Danny Skyfeather

# Practice #1:
## Breathing the Energy of Love

This is a crucial practice of this work. The second practice involves dropping the energy-infused heart-commands and affirmations into our subconscious minds and bodies. It is based on language. Words are powerful. They shape our lives.

However, there are places in our psyche, in our minds and bodies and memories, where words cannot reach. The energy of love travels to these places in us where intellect and language cannot go. Love reaches the pre-verbal places in our childhoods and the places in us that are irrational and beyond the reach of memory. That is why it is so important to do this self-love energy session every day.

This session involves taking deep and continuous breaths while holding the intention of transmitting the universal energy of love into the deepest reaches of our subconscious minds, bodies, emotions, and memories. We are literally pouring this energy of love into every crack, crevice, and corner of our beings. It may be a good idea to first read the instructions below multiple times and practice as you go along to get the method firmly implanted within you.

When I speak of "love" I don't necessarily mean the emotion of love, be it romantic or otherwise, although the emotional aspect of love is a part of the greater field of love. I am speaking of transpersonal and transcendent love. I am speaking of the universal *energy* that is equally and wholly present in all moments of time and space.

Love is the most healing, potent, and attractive force in the universe. It is intelligent, and knows exactly where to go inside us, what needs to be transformed, in what order, and according to what is in our best and highest good. When we send this energy into the deepest recesses of our beings, we are clearing out all sorts of old programs, beliefs, thoughts, and frozen trauma. Love is a very high vibration and cannot coexist in the same body and mind with energies that are lower and denser. The lower energies have to leave, heal, or transform.

This intelligent energy will do all this in ways that are the least painful and uncomfortable. Of course, there will be stuff that needs to come up to the conscious surface of our minds to be processed. We can't get around that. But there will also be copious amounts of material that will be healed and cleared without us ever being consciously aware of it.

This work requires emotional courage. When stuff gets stirred up and you don't know quite how to handle or process it, then reach out for help. Talk to someone. Ask a friend to just listen to you without interruption, advice, or judgement. If you are in a recovery group, then hit a few more meetings. Take a walk. Sit under a tree with your bare feet on the ground. Let the earth support you as you continue to love yourself and crawl out of past conditioning.

If the spiritual terms and descriptions don't resonate with you – and you come from a more agnostic perspective – then simply take deep and continuous breaths while holding the intention that love will travel through your hands and into the deepest layers of your mind and body. Breath + intention + love – that's all you need.

**Breathing the love**

This method of channeling love through your mind and body is simple and enjoyable. Here are the parts to this process that all work together in synergistic harmony:

*Medulla Oblongata.* This is the spiritual and energetic space at the back of your head and the base of your skull. It is right where the spine meets the skull. Ancient mystics call this space the "Mouth of God." I also like to call it the "escape hatch into Spirit."

*The inner eye.* This space is directly between your eyebrows and in the middle of your forehead, but slightly elevated. This is a place of intention, inner strength, and concentration. It is the command center of the mind, heart, and body. Focusing on this space activates your prefrontal cortex. Together, the medulla and the inner eye comprise your sixth chakra. Both the inner eye and the medulla are also connected to your heart-field in a triangle like shape.

*The heart-field.* This is located directly in the center of the chest. It is a vast, mysterious, and beautiful field of intelligent energy. It is our feeling center. It is where we express and receive compassion and empathy. It is simultaneously connected to all parts of our conscious, subconscious, and unconscious minds. It is also a riverbed of love. Through our heart-fields we can instantly transmit love to any place, any person, and to any time in the universe.

*The hands.* The hands are broadcasting stations of energy and love. They are intimately interwoven on an energetic level with the heart-field, the inner eye, and the medulla oblongata. They work together with the above three parts to concentrate and channel the vibration of love.

*Using those four parts together, let's begin...*

*Prepare.* Pick a length of time for the session. Starting with twenty-minutes is great. Using a timer is a good way to hold the energetic container. Make sure you won't be disturbed. Sit or lay back in a comfortable position. *Place one open hand on the center of your chest and another open hand on your belly.* In this way, you will be directing all the love back into your body and into all levels of your subconscious mind.

*Ask for help.* Start by inviting your higher self into your space. This is the highest, most evolved version of yourself on a spiritual level. Further ask and invite any spiritual masters, teachers, angels, or archetypes that resonate in the frequency of love to be present with you as well.

*Intention.* With all the inner power and resolve within you, set and hold the intention that the energy of pure intelligent love will flow into your body and mind throughout the length of your session.

*Start.* Begin breathing in long, deep, and continuous cycles – in and out of your nose. Allow no pauses between your inhaling and exhaling breaths. Fill and empty your belly and chest completely. Try to stretch out each inhale and exhale for as long as possible. Keep your eyes open or closed. Breathing in this way might be uncomfortable for the first few minutes. Keep going and you will acclimate.

*Nose or mouth.* Breathing through your nose purifies and conditions the air you take in. It also helps activate your inner eye and prefrontal cortex. It stimulates your imagination and helps focus your intention. That is why nose breathing is encouraged. However, this isn't a rigid rule. Choose whatever rhythm of nose/mouth breathing that you prefer. What is most important is your loving intention.

*Focused and relaxed concentration.* As you breathe in this deep and deliberate way, do your best to hold your awareness within your inner eye, between your eyebrows, and directly in the center of your forehead. Keep your body as relaxed as you can, and when your mind wanders, gently bring it back to this space. From this point of focused and relaxed concentration, also bring your awareness to *both* your heart-center and your medulla oblongata.

*During each long inhaling breath.* Stretch open and pull your heart-field up through your expanding medulla and into the higher dimensions of energy, consciousness, and love. Your medulla and heart-field are expanding and rising in unison. You could also imagine and intend that your heart-center rises to be above your head. For this reason, you could call this "heart-ascended breathing."

*During each long exhaling breath.* Flood the energy of love down through the top of your head, through your hands, into every cell and atom of your body, and into all your thoughts, memories, and emotions. Relax completely. You are loving yourself from a higher perspective. You are concentrating all the love in the entire universe into the deepest layers and levels of your own mind and body – conscious and subconscious.

Keep reminding yourself to breathe deeply with no pauses between your inhaling and exhaling breaths. *This session is all for you.* Do your best to crowd out all the concerns for others and what their needs are. This is *your time* to give yourself divine unconditional love.

Pour love into every moment, memory, age, phase, and into every corner of your life, mind, and body. When your mind wanders, just keep bringing it back to directing the energy of love into yourself.

Practice seeing and looking in on your human self from a higher level. You are raising your heart-center's energy and awareness to be above your body – where you are continuously giving yourself love for everything you are feeling and going through in any moment. All the hang-ups, emotions, triggers, idiosyncrasies, challenging habits, old beliefs, all of it – the so-called "good" and "bad" – are being bathed in the holy flow of divine and unconditional love. As you keep breathing, a waterfall of love will be continuously pouring into all levels of your body and mind.

This love will just keep flowing, and you can relax your focus on what's happening with each inhale and exhale. As best you can, stay single-pointedly focused on love. Stay relaxed. Let go into this flow. Allow yourself to be the channel of love for the benefit of your own sweet self.

*To recap.* With each inhaling breath, pull your ever-widening heart-center up through your expanding medulla and into Infinite Spirit. With each exhaling breath, flood the energy of love through your body, mind, and hands – and into yourself. Relax. Keep breathing. Let the love flow. This energy is touching and immediately benefitting everything contained in your mind and body. It is reaching all the places where language and words cannot reach. You are flooding yourself with much needed love, presence, compassion, understanding, and grace.

Again, if the above explanations are too wordy, feel free to forget all of it. Instead, simply take deep and continuous breaths while holding the intention that the energy of love will flood through your hands and into your mind and body. Again, breath + intention + love – that's all you need.

That is the basic method. The practice is to do one or two love-channeling sessions per day. A daily 20-minute session is a great place to start. This creates great healing momentum.

## 12-breath reboot

In addition to doing longer breathing/energy sessions on yourself every day – it is also a great idea to do periodic 12-breath reboots throughout the day. To do this, simply place your hands on your heart and belly. Close your eyes and take 12 deep, continuous, and love-channeling breaths as described above.

When you are done, relax your breath and enjoy the flow of love. This will "reboot" your mind and body to the flow of love through you while bringing you back to higher levels of energy and functioning. A great time to do a 12-breath reboot is before you fall asleep and when you wake up.

## Widen the circle

You can also widen the circle in which the love flows. To do this, take deep and continuous breaths and channel the love in the manner described above. As the love is flowing, imagine that a circle is drawn around your body in a circumference of about 12 feet. Then hold the intention that the energy of love is flooding into this space in a more intense and bigger broadcast of energy.

## The core self-love heart-command

You can also repeat the core heart command as you do your breathing sessions:

*I flood the energy of love through my mind and body*
*in all moments – and I open deeper to receive*
*and give this love to all life everywhere.*

# Practice #2:
# Breathing the Heart-Commands of Unconditional Self-Love

The Heart-Commands of Unconditional Self-Love are affirmations that are spoken with sincerity, feeling, intensity, and passion from the center of our chests and bodies. They are infused with the life-force energy of love for the immediate benefit of all who work them into our hearts, minds and bodies. The practice is to use your deliberate, continuous, and creative breath to literally inhale the essence, energy, and truth of these statements on deep, energetic, subtle, and subconscious levels.

This breath-reading method really works in getting these statements lodged into your subconscious intelligence, which is the part of your mind that represents your autopilot. It drives your car, does the dishes, and brushes your teeth, etc. As the commands get repeatedly lodged and reinforced within this part of the mind, they will begin to sink down into the deeper underbelly, or unconscious mind, just like water sinks into soil. Using this method, we transcend our need to consciously *comprehend* so that we can subconsciously and superconsciously *apprehend* and *GET* them.

## Breathing the commands

This is an amazingly simple method of rapidly absorbing the energy-infused statements, commands, and affirmations in this book. However, it still requires a fair amount of practice to master.

The simplest explanation of this method is as follows: take long, deep and continuous breaths as you rapidly skim your mind over the affirmations – all while holding the intention that your heart-center and higher intelligence are rapidly absorbing their essence and truth.

Beyond that, here are some more detailed insights into this practice...

*Deep, even, and continuous breaths.* Breathe all the way in and all the way out. Raise your heart-field up with each inhale and open the flow of divine and unconditional love through your mind and body. As you do, concentrate your awareness into the space between your eyebrows and the center of your forehead. From here, also intend and imagine that your heart-center is opening and expanding in its own beautiful way.

*Rapidly move over the words.* Once you have your breath rolling, rapidly move your mind's awareness over the words in a "speed reading" type of way. Dance over them in a smooth but speedy manner. Let-go of the need to consciously read every word with your thinking brain. Go through a full page in 10 to 20 seconds.

*Keep your head still.* If you find your head moving back and forth, then just relax it and keep it as still as possible. Moving it back and forth is sending a body message of saying "no" to what you are taking in. However, if you keep your head still and your eyes dancing back and forth over the words, then you are tapping into the resources in both hemispheres of your brain.

*Spiritual eye.* Imagine and intend that the spiritual space in the center of your forehead is rapidly highlighting the words in a way as to take them in on an energetic and essence level. Stay focused on this area. Burn your forehead to the page.

*Heart-center.* As you breathe and keep your mind focused on your spiritual eye, hold the intention that your heart-center is opening, expanding, inhaling, absorbing, assimilating, and anchoring the energetic essence and truth of the self-love commands on a body-based level directly into your nervous system and subconscious mind. It is like your energetic heart-field is reaching out and hugging the words, digesting them emotionally, and planting them directly into the deepest layers of your body and mind – all while bypassing the need to read every word with the conscious thinking brain.

*The conscious mind.* As you do this, your conscious mind will attempt to slow down and start reading the words. It likes to be in control. The challenge is to just keep rapidly skimming as you breathe deeply and continuously. In this way, there is

Danny Skyfeather

no time for the conscious mind to reject and criticize what you are absorbing on an energetic level.

*Concentrate.* Do your best to hold the *intense intention* that you are rapidly absorbing the commands with heightened spiritual and superconscious concentration. Do your best to crowd out the tendency to think of other things as you do this.

*Challenges.* It can be a challenge to keep breathing deeply while also moving rapidly across the page. You might find that you stop breathing deeply, or that you slow down the pace that your awareness is moving across the page. When this happens, just pick up the pace again.

*Eyes.* It is important to relax your eyes and the muscles that surround them. Soften your gaze. The point is just to move your *relaxed gaze* across the words in a rapid way as you breathe continuously while keeping your attention on your prefrontal cortex and heart-center.

*Superconscious mind.* Reach for a higher and spiritual absorption of the commands by staying focused on the center of your forehead and the intention of embedding them into your heart-center. As you do, you will know it when you reach that level of lucid focus and concentration. It isn't a place of mentally and consciously reading the words in a typical way, and it isn't just casually skimming either. It is a clear, high, calm, and efficient absorbing of the commands.

*Send the love.* As you are breathing and skimming, also hold the intention of channeling the highest energy of love into the words that your mind is dancing across. Send the love for your own benefit, and for the benefit of everyone else rapidly absorbing the affirmations in this way.

*Taking in the whole energy field.* With this rapid skimming and deep breathing method, you are really tapping into the whole essence, energy, and truth of the heart-commands of self-love that are contained there. You are tapping into the energetic mastermind aspect of this book. Your heart is connecting with all beings who are doing the same thing in all times and places. Do your best to feel the energy of love that everyone else is sending into these pages. Feel how good it feels to know that your love is reaching everyone else as well. You are tapping into this book as a wave of energy and consciousness instead of just a collection of words organized in a certain way.

*When finished.* Once you have gone through the entire group of heart-commands, close your eyes and relax. Place a hand on your heart, keep breathing deeply for a moment or two and notice how all of the heart-commands are imprinted in your consciousness. Feel and intend that they all sink deeply into your heart-center, emotional and energetic centers, and into your body and subconscious mind.

*Continuity of practice.* When you do this every single day, coming back again and again, your subconscious mind and your higher-than-conscious intelligence will be reinforcing and taking them in on even deeper levels. It really starts to accumulate and accelerate after a few days and weeks of this. The more you practice, the better you will get at it, and it's impossible to do it wrong.

*Stuff can come up.* Keep in mind also that stuff can come up that is uncomfortable to feel. This means that the affirmations and the energy of love that is transmitted through them are moving stuff around and clearing it out. Healing is taking place. During these times of alchemical upheaval, take extra care of yourself. Talk to a friend. Take a hike in nature. Plant your bare feet on the ground. Take a nap. Take a bath. Go to yoga. Do what is necessary to send yourself a signal that you care about your own well-being.

*Healing music.* To enhance this practice, do this method while listening to any type of healing or meditation music.

*Mind-Chest Tapping.* You can also incorporate this tapping method into your practice of breathing the commands.

*Try it now.* Go to page 61 and try this method. See how it feels. Get your own rhythm of *breath-speed-reading* going.

~~~

Go through all the heart-commands at least once per day in this heightened and energetic way. You can also read and speak them in a slower way. Repeating them out-loud while tapping the center of your chest with an open hand is a good supplemental practice.

This method works for any spiritual book that is hard to get on a conscious thinking level, but that you really want to absorb into the deepest levels of your subconscious and unconscious minds. It works great for books of affirmations and for spiritual texts. It is not necessary to fully understand the material on a conscious level in order to plant it into the vast intelligence of our subconscious minds. *We can intuitively absorb and apprehend what is hard for us to consciously understand and comprehend.* Our deeper intelligence can read, assimilate, take in, and act upon massive amounts of words, energy, and information in a short period of time.

As you breathe these commands every day, powerfully intend that you are anchoring them into your bone marrow, and into your nerves, muscles, tissues, blood, cells, DNA, and atoms. Point them within. Repeat and vibrate them with your entire body. Every tiny part of your body and mind gets to feel and accept them. They will help shift, move, and transmute old material from within you. Your health, life, and relationships will improve. Every aspect of your life will get better. It does take time, however.

The beauty of this process is that we are breathing, feeling and absorbing them together. As we heart-anchor and vibrate them within our bodies and minds, we do so for our individual and mutual benefit.

Danny Skyfeather

# Practice #3:
# Unconditional Self-Love Mirror Work

Mirror work is extraordinarily powerful in building a positive self-image, self-esteem, and a genuine inner state of self-love. As simple as this practice is, it can also be difficult to stick to. I have gone months of doing mirror work every night, and then fell off the self-love train and didn't do it for a very long time, and then picked up the practice again. The idea is to be kind and gentle with ourselves when we fall out of a healthy practice. That inner kindness is the fuel to get back up again.

Here is the basics of doing mirror work: For around two minutes in the morning and evening, look into your own eyes in the mirror. Really look with a penetrating gaze of love. Take deep heart-expanding breaths and energetically broadcast the energy of love through your heart and into the eyes and heart of the beautiful soul looking back at you. Maintain eye contact with yourself the whole time. This isn't a time for teeth brushing or focusing on facial blemishes, etc. Keep this time as a sacred commitment to love yourself unconditionally.

You can also take this time to gently and continuously tap your chest with an open hand as you repeat, feel, and vibrate the core heart-command multiple times from the center of your chest:

*I flood the energy of love through my mind and body*
*in all moments – and I open deeper to receive*
*and give this love to all life everywhere.*

Take several deep love-channeling breaths before and after each repetition. Maintain eye contact with yourself as you repeat it. Speak with sincerity, feeling, and passionate intensity, even if you have to fake it in the beginning. Feel free to also repeat any other affirmations or heart-commands during this time.

At first, doing mirror work may feel awkward and strange, and you might fight against doing it. The practice is to just do it anyway. Do. It. Anyway. The intention is to establish a loving and heart-felt connection with your beautiful self. Make it a practice. The first few days or weeks may be hard. However, once you get past a few weeks, it will get easier.

Doing short mirror work sessions throughout the day can also keep your self-love flowing. When the screens of our phones and tablets are off, they act as excellent mirror surfaces.

## Practice #4:
## Self-Care of Body, Mind, and Environment

### Clean eating

What we eat is a direct reflection of our internal state of self-love or lack thereof. Spoken in another way: eating food that is unhealthy totally counteracts any efforts at positive change, self-affirmation, or transformation. It's really hard to poison our bodies with toxic food and love ourselves at the same time. In short, *food sobriety* is a crucial ingredient in loving ourselves unconditionally.

I know that is true for myself. During times in my life where I am hard on myself, and the old self-hatred programs are running the show, I eat tons of junk food. My goal when I am in this state is to stop feeling anything, to bury myself under a comfortable layer of belly fat. Early in childhood I discovered that over-eating was a very efficient way to mask painful emotions. When I was eating, chewing, and swallowing – I was distracted from the inner turmoil, self-hatred, terror, and emotional pain raging inside me. The only problem was that once the act of eating was over, the pain came back.

Alternatively, when I am making a concerted and daily effort to love and honor myself on the deepest levels of my being, I blend a lot of raw vegetable smoothies and keep a regular schedule of time that I eat and time when I don't eat anything at all.

This book is not intended in any way to preach or attempt to tell people what to eat and not to eat. I will not walk into that minefield. However, I do feel a need and desire to simply share my experience. You are free to take what you can use and leave the rest.

For me, whole food and plant-based eating combined with intermittent fasting works the best. A structure that I like to keep is this: drink raw vegetable blended smoothies from 10 am to 2 pm, then eat solid food until 5 pm, and then eat nothing until the next day at 10 am.

When we give our bodies long breaks from digesting food, our cells have room and freedom to assimilate, purge old material, and create new cells. This schedule works for me. Everyone has their own definition of what works.

I have done many multiple day juice fasts and blends, and I am always thrilled at the level of mental and emotional clarity that I can reach when I am in a clean eating state. Clear foods create clear feelings and thoughts. I have also fallen out of more juice fasts and plans than I have successfully completed. It isn't easy, at least for me.

If I am constantly thinking about junk food that I want to eat, while depriving myself from them, then I am more likely to fail. It is better to want healthy food and consistently *add them* to my daily consumption than to want unhealthy food and *deprive myself* of them. To add is better than to take away. However, there are many times that my unhealthy eating habits have been so ingrained that I need to lay down the gauntlet and stop eating them altogether for a period of time, all while adding the positive foods.

What I really found was that the thoughts I think during these periods of clean eating make a huge difference in my success. When I am thinking positive thoughts, and cultivating empowered states of emotion, then staying with clean eating is much easier.

A major intention of this book is for it to be a support for people who are attempting a radical change in diet and lifestyle. Whether you are doing raw vegetable blends every day, or are embarking on a 40-day juice fast, or any other type of healthy shift in eating – then repeating and anchoring thoughts of self-love within your heart-field is a great way to stay committed. Just like you slam your green smoothie, breathe the affirmations in this book every day as well. It is just as important to consume loving thoughts about yourself than to consume healthy, vibrant, and living food. Doing both is optimal.

What does clean eating mean to you? If you don't know already, I encourage you to find what works for you. Each of us are different, and approach food differently. A body and mind that is brimming over with clear energy is more able to absorb and act upon positive statements and affirmations.

In short, a huge and integral way to love yourself is to love your body through the foods you eat. The self-love commands and affirmations in this book will help you stick with healthy eating, and healthy eating will help you stay with this process of anchoring these commands into your mind and body.

## Water

Drinking copious amounts of clean water is a profound act of self-love. It seems so simple, but it's enormously helpful to drink as much as you can to keep your cells hydrated. Being amply hydrated also helps you process emotions with more grace and efficiency.

A great practice is to paste a copy of the core heart-command (or other affirmations) on the outside of your water bottle. Before you take a drink, hold the bottle between your hands and channel the energy of love into all the water molecules. Your water will then be charged with the energy of love. This love-charged water will penetrate deep into your cells and compliment this process in a major way.

## Exercise

Exercising feels good afterward. However, at least for me, I never feel like exercising. I am often tired, groggy, yawny, and not in the mood. So it takes a good amount of inner-oomph to get up and get moving. I always need to remind myself that self-love means getting off the couch to exercise even when I don't want to. Self-love is doing all the healthy stuff I don't feel like doing. Gentle self-discipline is self-love.

When we are exercising, we are sending a signal to every cell in our bodies that we care for our physical health. During your journey of energetic self-love, I encourage you to find an exercise routine that works well for you.

Walking is one of the very best forms of exercise. Getting more intense with a gym membership and a personal trainer might be just what you need as well. Yoga is also a great modality to unearth and clear out old emotional energy stored in the body.

A big component to exercise is having fun. For me, when I play basketball, it gives my inner child a chance to have a blast. I feel so much joy running around the court with younger athletes. Sometimes I feel like I might explode with joy. What type of exercise and body movement brings you joy? There are so many to choose from. Find one.

## Environment

As a child growing up, I never really learned how to care for myself by caring for my environment. A great self-love barometer is how messy my house is. The outer reflects the inner. Perhaps you could take the time to clear out stuff you don't need or want anymore. Sometimes self-love means just washing the dishes.

Keep in mind also that everyone is different in this regard. Some people are hyper-controlling and their environment reflects inner rigidity by being over clean. Others are looser and a messy environment reflects inner chaos. The point here is to become more aware and strive to create an outer environment that reflects your inner self-love.

# Heart-Commands of
# Unconditional Self-Love

Danny Skyfeather

Welcome to the Heart-Commands of Unconditional Self-Love. In this section, you are invited to use the method described in Practice #2 above to anchor them rapidly and energetically into your heart-center, cells, body, and all levels of your subconscious and unconscious minds. Making this a daily practice will ignite your process.

*Here is a short recap of that method*: Take deep, smooth, and continuous breaths. As you do, focus intensely on your inner eye between your eyebrows and in the center of your forehead, and on opening and expanding your heart-center. Keep your head still. Relax your eyes and the muscles around them as you rapidly move your awareness across the words. Soften your gaze. Feel and intend that your heart-field is opening, expanding, inhaling, absorbing, anchoring, and energetically assimilating the truth, essence, and energy of the heart-commands. As you breathe these affirmations, also transmit your highest love into them for the greatest good of yourself and everyone who is absorbing them in this way.

## The Core Heart-Command of Unconditional Self-Love

Throughout the following section, this core heart-command will be repeated at regular intervals as an anchoring affirmation. Having it spaced apart in this manner is intentional, as spaced repetition of heart-felt affirmations make them more effective. Each time you see, breathe, and energetically vibrate it within your consciousness, it will become a more deeply rooted reality within you.

*I flood the energy of love through my mind and body*
*in all moments – and I open deeper to receive*
*and give this love to all life everywhere.*

This affirmational command of the heart helps you be the eagle of divine consciousness that is showering every moment of your life with unconditional love. It is most effective when repeated, felt, and reverberated on an emotional level via the energetic heart.

A simple but effective practice is to repeat it while you are tapping your chest in a rhythmic way with an open hand. As you do, feel and intend that you are tapping the words themselves into the center of your chest and directly into your subconscious mind. This core affirmation is also the second command in my other book, *Heart-Commands of Awakened Love*.

This command has several intentions built into it. *First*, it points and anchors you into your highest and most elevated consciousness and accesses the flow of love through your mind and body. *Second*, it invokes the emotional courage to accept and receive the love you are giving yourself. *Third*, it is allowing this love to pass through you to benefit all of life.

## Mind-Chest Tapping

For even more amazing results, do a few rounds of Mind-Chest Tapping before and after you do your *breath-speed-reading*. This will help plant and reinforce these commands within your subconscious mind even more.

# Heart-Commands of Unconditional Self-Love

*I flood the energy of love through my mind and body*
*in all moments – and I open deeper to receive*
*and give this love to all life everywhere.*

Immersed in the infinite love that I am – I love myself wholly and unconditionally. I love myself radically, fiercely, and gently. With every expanding breath I take, I fall more in love with my very own being. I hold myself in high esteem and embrace myself in waves of light. Every day in every way – my self-love grows stronger.

I speak these heart-commands of self-love with increasing passion and vibrational intensity. I speak them with such internal power that my bodily cells shake and vibrate. I speak them with such soul-force that all life feels their truth. I saturate these statements with spiritualized emotion – allowing them entry into my body and subconscious mind.

*I flood the energy of love through my mind and body*
*in all moments – and I open deeper to receive*
*and give this love to all life everywhere.*

Love is the core truth of my being. The highest love that I am is now wholly awake and manifest within and as every cell and atom of my body and mind. I am growing in the sunlight of awakened love.

I am crafted from the perfect energy of love. I am one with this Infinite Source of Love. I am grateful to know myself as the very essence of love. I love myself from the place where consciousness creates reality.

*I flood the energy of love through my mind and body*
*in all moments – and I open deeper to receive*
*and give this love to all life everywhere.*

I visualize a higher version of myself sitting before me. I see myself with as much detail as possible. I take long, deep, and continuous breaths – giving and receiving the energy of love with myself. Breathing in, I receive love. Breathing out, I give love.

Mutually flowing rivers of love connect our heart-centers. I imagine, intend, and feel this love flowing into and from my higher self. I plant this image into my chest and see it growing in clarity every day.

*I flood the energy of love through my mind and body*
*in all moments – and I open deeper to receive*
*and give this love to all life everywhere.*

Anchored in supreme joy – I love myself unconditionally. My self-love grows with every passing minute, hour, and day. Within and beyond my conscious awareness – my self-love continues to expand.

I am joined on a silent level with all beautiful souls across time and space who are anchoring these affirmations into our minds and bodies. I am grateful for this innate connection of love with all others on this planet who are doing this work.

I am committed to taking good care of my body, mind, and spirit. I place a warm hand of love upon my chest and give myself encouragement, compassion, and kindness. I am my own divine lover. Every day, my subconscious mind populates my awareness with even more creative thoughts of self-love.

*I flood the energy of love through my mind and body*
*in all moments – and I open deeper to receive*
*and give this love to all life everywhere.*

I am loved, lovable, and loving. I am the innocence of love. In every moment, I bathe myself in benevolent understanding. I meet all my emotional needs for connection, inclusion, and community from within.

I am infinitely blessed by the waterfall of energetic love perpetually cascading through every crevice of my mind and body. I am emotionally fed from the flowing waters of my soul.

I genuinely love all the moments and stages of my life. From birth to death, I fiercely love my entire life. I am the divine love inhabiting all moments of my journey – and I am the human being stepping with courage into every new stage of my life.

*I flood the energy of love through my mind and body*
*in all moments – and I open deeper to receive*
*and give this love to all life everywhere.*

I wrap my arms of immortal light around my inner child. Every day, I am more in tune with my inner child. My inner child is so bright, beautiful, innocent, and free. I pour the essence of love into every moment of my childhood.

I nurture my child self. I honor and protect my innocence. I cherish my vulnerable heart. I give myself permission to be seen by those I trust. In my own time and wisdom, I allow another piece of armor around my heart to fall away. I look upon my soft and open heart with eyes of gentle compassion.

Anchored in my own worth, I allow myself to grow and contribute in authentic and beautiful ways. I am the mother and father of my own greatest potential.

*I flood the energy of love through my mind and body*
*in all moments – and I open deeper to receive*
*and give this love to all life everywhere.*

I adore the miracle of my birth. I gently hold and wrap my baby self in pure love. I see an image of myself as an adult holding my newborn self. I bathe this image in love and anchor it further within my emotional centers.

*I flood the energy of love through my mind and body*
*in all moments – and I open deeper to receive*
*and give this love to all life everywhere.*

I work daily to build a self-image of love toward myself. I envision a waterfall of unconditional love cascading down, through and all around my body and mind. It encircles me in a 12-foot radius. I visualize this circle with as much detail as possible. This flow of love continues in the hours, days, weeks, and years to come – on levels that include and transcend my conscious awareness. The image of this waterfall keeps growing more vivid within me. My self-image creates my life.

My higher intelligence continues to create more internal images of love and respect toward myself. As these images come to my awareness, I plant them into the soil of my heart and mind. I water them daily with my care and attention.

*I flood the energy of love through my mind and body*
*in all moments – and I open deeper to receive*
*and give this love to all life everywhere.*

I breathe open my heart of love – and I love others as myself. I dedicate the love I give myself to the greater good of all life. Self-love heals the world. I do my part by loving my entire being with persistence and loyalty. The love I give myself grows as beautiful flowers in the hearts and minds of other human beings.

I am energetically intwined with universal love. I have never been anywhere but in the light of love. From this heightened perspective – I love my eyes, face, and mouth. I love my knees, legs, arms, back, fingers, hands, feet, and toes. I love every organ, muscle, tissue, cell, protein, molecule, and DNA strand of my body. I bathe my trillions of cells in the brilliant joy of love.

Danny Skyfeather

Even though doing this work can be difficult, I've got this. Anchored in love, I am stronger than my pain and stronger than my past. I enfold every wound and trauma within me in the healing power of love. I love everything that arises from within.

My innocence transcends and heals my trauma. I allow the light of my innocence to touch the face of what hurts within me. As I do, I experience profound healing and a true awakening of wholeness.

*I flood the energy of love through my mind and body*
*in all moments – and I open deeper to receive*
*and give this love to all life everywhere.*

I practice gentle self-discipline. I get up and get moving. I do what needs to be done. I am an adult to myself. I care for my body, mind, and environment in the clearest and highest way possible. I deserve to be cared for – and it is my job to practice this self-care. I nurture the health of my body, mind, and environment.

I embrace my emotions with ever-increasing love. I accept myself for how I feel. My emotions are beautiful. I invite all my emotions to gently melt into the river of love flowing through the kingdoms of my innermost being.

I am the love that transcends my human experience. I am the love that descends into the fragmented emotions and memories of my mind and body. I process all emotional pain from a heightened place of love, joy, and gratitude.

*I flood the energy of love through my mind and body*
*in all moments – and I open deeper to receive*
*and give this love to all life everywhere.*

I practice self-honesty and self-awareness. To be honest with myself is to love myself. Whenever I step out of self-love, I immediately practice self-gentleness and guide myself back to the path of growth. I am my own best friend.

I radically forgive myself. I absolve myself for all past mistakes. I breathe forgiveness into myself. I broadcast self-forgiveness to every cell of my body. All prisoners of thought held in the cages of shame are released. Self-forgiveness guides the forgotten parts of me to the center of my chest. They have a seat waiting for them at the harvest table of love and joy. May they feast, laugh, cry, and feel at home. All of me is embraced in love.

*I flood the energy of love through my mind and body
in all moments – and I open deeper to receive
and give this love to all life everywhere.*

I am a delightful and beautiful human being. I celebrate and appreciate myself. As I practice self-love every day, I can be real and vulnerable with someone that I trust. Rooted in self-love, I experience a greater energy of love. I am safe in the arms of eternal love.

These thoughts sink into the intelligence of my heart-field. I accept these thoughts as my truth on the subconscious level of my mind. I intend that they penetrate and grow from the depths of my unconscious mind. They are further received and acted upon by my highest spiritual intelligence. These heart-commands of self-love are the supreme law of my entire being. They become more real and manifest every day.

*I flood the energy of love through my mind and body
in all moments – and I open deeper to receive
and give this love to all life everywhere.*

Danny Skyfeather

I believe in myself. I believe in my heart, in my ideas, and in my dreams. I believe in my greatest potential. It is my sole responsibility to believe in myself. Even during moments of heartache or pain – I never stop believing in me. This faith in myself will continue to grow in all the moments of my life to come.

I wrap all my seeming failures in the light of kindness. I allow myself to make mistakes and give myself compassion amid those mistakes. For the large and small mistakes, I love and forgive myself. I gently encourage myself to keep walking, to never give up, and to see the true blessings in all my stumbles and setbacks. I am a beautiful human and spiritual being. I am okay just as I am – and I improve with each step I take. Life is good – and I am good. I am committed to loving myself through every life experience. I am my greatest champion.

I love myself for being alive. With an expanding breath, I relax into the energy of love within me. My own soft and eternal love is my safe place to land. The center of my chest opens wider with every breath I take – as my thoughts rest in the gentle embrace of energetic love.

*I flood the energy of love through my mind and body*
*in all moments – and I open deeper to receive*
*and give this love to all life everywhere.*

Breathing in – my heart, mind, and body opens into a broad and beautiful smile. Breathing out – I turn that smile inward upon myself. I smile light into every cell, thought, and emotion within me. Every second of my life is a reason to smile. I smile into myself every day. I savor the sweet joy of my own existence. I am grateful to be alive. I am grateful to love myself even more. To love myself is to love the universe – as the universe is enfolded within me.

*I flood the energy of love through my mind and body*
*in all moments – and I open deeper to receive*
*and give this love to all life everywhere.*

I hold myself and this planet within my heart-space of unconditional love. With my deliberate imagination – I choose to witness, envision, and create a free, peaceful, and abundant world for all of life.

Placing a hand upon my chest – I send waves of love to humanity and the earth. I call to the vibration of love within me to rise. Every day, I resonate in higher and more harmonious states of joy, health and radiance. As my vibration rises, the world is a better place to live.

*I flood the energy of love through my mind and body*
*in all moments – and I open deeper to receive*
*and give this love to all life everywhere.*

My relationships are built upon the sacred ground of unconditional self-love. In my relationships, I feel and say: *I love myself, I love you, I love myself, and I love you.* I teach other people how to treat me. As I love and value myself, other people do the same.

I allow myself to experience raw and beautiful intimacy with another heart and soul. The truth is that I deserve to be loved without condition. I give this love to myself first. Immersed in my own love, I trust the love from others. I am truly worthy of love and connection.

*I flood the energy of love through my mind and body*
*in all moments – and I open deeper to receive*
*and give this love to all life everywhere.*

Danny Skyfeather

It is safe for me to love and be loved in return – and I love the part of me that is afraid of love. This part deserves my compassion, gentleness, and kindness the most. I hold the frightened parts of my being in the hands of my highest love. It is safe for me to love and be loved in return.

I superconsciously flood my subconscious mind with love. This energy is performing miracles for me on levels beyond my conscious awareness. Love knows what to cleanse, clear, and heal within me – all with infinite grace and precision.

I now call forth the elevated emotional states of love, joy, awe, wonder, enthusiasm, gratitude, freedom, peace, and delight to rise within me. I activate the innate intelligence of my heart-field to bring all these elevated emotions into full feeling and expression. These emotions support my physical health, my emotional well-being, and my state of mind. Joy is my birthright. It is my human right to feel good. I always have direct access to elevated emotions.

*I flood the energy of love through my mind and body*
*in all moments – and I open deeper to receive*
*and give this love to all life everywhere.*

I bathe my body, mind, and heart in rivers of liquid joy. Ever-new and increasing joy is cascading through the center of my chest. I am a dynamo of joy in service to the highest awakening of joy everywhere. I move my life into my greatest joy, even if it means the dissolution of my comfort zones. I generously sacrifice the familiar in favor of the magnificent.

*I flood the energy of love through my mind and body*
*in all moments – and I open deeper to receive*
*and give this love to all life everywhere.*

I love myself by affirming that my essential nature is love. At the core of my being, I am love. I rest in the love I am and enjoy the flow of love. I am the highest consciousness of love and a channel through which love travels. I am both.

I am patient with myself as I experience upward cycles of growth, renewal, and awakening. I practice persistence over time. I deserve a mind and body that reflects the highest love for myself and all life.

*I flood the energy of love through my mind and body*
*in all moments – and I open deeper to receive*
*and give this love to all life everywhere.*

I give myself the energy of unconditional peace. Peace to my *belly*. Peace to my *heart*. Peace to my *body*. Peace to my *mind*. I deserve peace of belly, heart, body, and mind. I choose peace for myself in this present moment.

I work to cultivate peace within me. I speak to myself with a soothing voice of kindness. I calm myself with gentle self-talk. It is my responsibility to create peace within me. I accept this responsibility now.

On the inner levels of thought and emotion – I end the war with myself. I declare peace within my mind and body. Peace is the prevailing law of my being. As I cultivate peace on the inner levels, my outer life will reflect this peace.

*I flood the energy of love through my mind and body*
*in all moments – and I open deeper to receive*
*and give this love to all life everywhere.*

I love and care for my physical body. I look within and ask my body: *How can I care for you even more?* Then I listen for the answer. I am grateful for the awe-inspiring intelligence of my bodily cells. I thank my body for the tireless work it does.

I ingest foods that are overflowing with life-force energy. My diet reflects an ongoing care for my body, emotions, heart, and mind. I strive to make elevated food choices. When I eat less than optimal food, I am gentle with myself. I return to healthier foods at my earliest opportunity.

Danny Skyfeather

*I flood the energy of love through my mind and body*
*in all moments – and I open deeper to receive*
*and give this love to all life everywhere.*

I love and honor my sacred voice. I appreciate what I have to express to this world. I give myself space to be heard. My voice is a beautiful instrument of love. Every day, my voice gets clearer and stronger.

I hold the intention that these heart-commands of self-love are rooting themselves deeper into my emotional and energetic bodies. They reach even further into all levels of my conscious, subconscious, unconscious, and superconscious minds.

The truth and power of unconditional and energetic self-love is growing inside me, on conscious levels, and on levels beyond my conscious awareness. In all the minutes, hours, days, and weeks to come – my genuine love for myself will continue to effortlessly grow and expand within me.

*I flood the energy of love through my mind and body*
*in all moments – and I open deeper to receive*
*and give this love to all life everywhere.*

With each intentional breath *in*, I raise my consciousness to the highest vibration of love. With each relaxing breath *out*, I pour the energy of this love down and through my skull, brain, shoulders, arms, legs, muscles, tissues, cells, and atoms. Every level of my being – conscious and unconscious – is bathed in this holy flow of love. As I love myself – I am loved by all. As I love all – I love myself.

Love cascades through me like a thundering waterfall, providing all that I need and more – then pouring inward to humanity and the world. I am grateful to be silently and energetically connected with all beautiful souls who are repeating these statements with me now.

It is my heart-activated intention that the energy of love flows perpetually through these commands of the heart for the highest and immediate good of all of us who are breathing, feeling, and energetically anchoring them within our minds and bodies – in all times and places. It is so.

*I flood the energy of love through my mind and body*
*in all moments – and I open deeper to receive*
*and give this love to all life everywhere.*

Danny Skyfeather

# Loving Ourselves in the Loving Presence of Each Other

Danny Skyfeather

# Unconditional Self-Love Meetings

You are free to start or attend any Unconditional Self-Love Meeting. You are also free NOT to. Meetings can be helpful but are not totally necessary. You can go through this work on your own, and then find a friend, counselor, priest, therapist, or confidant to share your story with.

At the same time, there can be great value in attending a meeting of this kind. When we show up and consciously love ourselves in a safe energetic container with other people, we tap into the strength that comes from being vulnerable. Please see these types of meetings as a complimentary way to connect with others to enhance your healing journey. What follows are suggestions for getting the most out of a group experience of this kind...

## Basic Structure

These meetings are different from traditional addiction recovery meetings. During meetings of this kind, we do 10 minutes of self-love energy breathing, repeat potent heart-commands of unconditional self-love, and then openly affirm our self-love in the presence of each other.

*Arrive and leave in silence.* To honor the integrity and energetic container of the group, it is strongly recommended to arrive and leave in silence. Chatting before and after the meeting really dissipates the potent intention of the meeting. If you want to connect and talk with others, wait until you have completely left the meeting.

*Start and stop on time.* This seems kind of rigid, but the energetic container is strengthened when the meeting starts and stops on time.

*Avoid cross-talk and offering advice.* Meetings of this kind are not opportunities to socialize, but more like opportunities to transform. We are using the collective energy of the group to deepen our individual practice. In this respect, it is really important to avoid cross-talk or offering advice during the meeting. Each person's share is sacred.

*Active and heart-centered listening and presence.* Step 12 involves offering our heart-felt listening presence to other people in their process. When other people are sharing, zoom in on them with your full presence. Listen with your eyes, your heart, and the energy of your body. Send the person who is sharing your silent waves of appreciation and support.

*Keep shares brief and self-affirmational.* The purpose of sharing in these meetings is to openly say how wonderful, good, fabulous, valuable, loving, and lovable you are. The purpose is to love yourself in the loving presence of others. If it is hard to love yourself, or you are going through periods of self-hatred, it is okay to share that. Sharing how hard it is to love yourself is a powerful statement of self-love. Also, do your best not to ramble. Stay intentional and as focused as you can.

## Suggested Meeting Format (The leader reads the following)

The purpose of Unconditional Self-Love Meetings is to practice self-love in the loving presence of each other. The intention of this meeting is to use the collective energy of the group to deepen our own practice of loving ourselves wholly, completely, and unconditionally. This meeting will last for one hour. We will practice breathing the energy of love through our minds and bodies for 10 minutes, then repeat heart-commands of self-love for 10 minutes, followed by brief periods of sharing where we openly and out-loud affirm our self-love.

Cross talk, offering unwanted advice, or crossing emotional boundaries are discouraged. It is paramount that we offer our full presence and listening hearts to each person who shares.

Further, please respect the privacy of everyone who attends this meeting. Who attends this meeting and what is spoken here needs to stay inside the container of this meeting.

Confidentiality is vitally important. However, this does not indicate a legal privilege, and any statements that indicate an intention of imminent harm to yourself or others are not private.

(Optionally read the 12 steps)

Here are the Twelve Steps of Unconditional Self-Love, spoken from the I AM affirmational perspective:

Step 1: I understand that the root cause of much of my suffering is a lack of self-love – and I realize that I need to begin loving myself.

Step 2: I believe that unconditionally loving myself will heal and transform my life.

Step 3: I now begin, continue, and deepen the sincere practice of energetic and unconditional self-love on a daily and persistent basis.

Step 4: I courageously write down where I have been in my life with the willingness to support, embrace, and love all earlier versions of myself.

Step 5: I tap into my vulnerability and share my story with another human being that I love and trust.

Step 6: I look honestly at my conditioned patterns from the deeper understanding that there is nothing wrong with me.

Step 7: I practice radical self-acceptance and self-forgiveness on the deepest levels of my body and mind.

Step 8: I come to understand how self-hatred has hurt myself, other human beings, and my relationships with them.

Step 9: I heal the damage that self-hatred has caused myself and others by building and strengthening a self-image of love toward myself.

Step 10: I practice self-awareness and self-honesty on a daily basis. When I step out of alignment with self-love, I gently guide myself back.

Step 11: Every day I reach for higher perspectives of inner growth. I enjoy ever-upward cycles of expansion that never end. I practice cultivating elevated emotional states of love, joy, awe, wonder, enthusiasm, gratitude, freedom, peace, and delight.

Step 12: I am committed to being present to support others in their process of unconditional self-love. As I hold space for others in loving themselves, I am loving myself on deeper and more fulfilling levels.

For 10 minutes, we will now practice breathing the energy of love through our minds and bodies... (Place one hand on your heart, and the other on your belly, and begin breathing the love).

(10 minutes)

We will now repeat affirmations and heart-commands of self-love. When you are listening, please hold your hand on your heart or gently and rhythmically tap your chest with an open hand as you breathe deeply and self-reflect the heart-commands into your heart, body, and mind. (Read from the heart-command section yourself or read a few paragraphs and pass to someone else to read. There is no need to get through the whole section.)

(10 minutes)

We will now offer short and potent shares where we affirm out-loud our unconditional self-love for ourselves. This is not a time to offer advice or counsel to others, but to speak thoughts of genuine self-love for ourselves in the loving presence of each other. You are free to share or pass.

(Start yourself or pick someone and go around the space. 2 to 3-minute shares are recommended to give everyone a chance to share).

(The end of the hour arrives)

We have now reached the end of our meeting. We will close by repeating the Core Heart-Command of Unconditional Self-Love:

*I flood the energy of love through my mind and body*
*in all moments – and I open deeper to receive*
*and give this love to all life everywhere.*

Depart in silence.

*notes:*

Danny Skyfeather

# Self-Love Partners and Intimate Relationships

## Self-Love Partners

There is value in doing this work with a close friend or self-love partner. This can be anyone who is committed to doing this work themselves and who also supports you in doing this work.

Working one-on-one with someone is not required or even necessary. Many people prefer to do this work solo. Also, just by working with this book you are connecting on a silent energetic level with everyone else doing this work. Having said all that, some people find great value in teaming up with others.

You can structure this type of connection in any way you choose. You can follow the meeting format above or adjust it according to your own preferences and desires. Here are some more suggestions...

*Have a regular schedule.* If you embark upon this type of journey with someone, have a regular time that you meet. This will increase the strength of your energetic container.

*Be honest and loving with each other.* The purpose of this type of connection is to be honest but loving with each other. Tell the other person the truth as you see it, all while offering them love and support to walk with them through the experience. Also, be willing to listen to the truth from the other person. Don't suck up to each other. Don't emotionally cover for each other. Avoid codependence as best you can. Maintain your own emotional autonomy.

*Trade listening time.* You can have a timer and trade listening time. This values both people in the relationship.

*When you are the one sharing.* Do your best to be real and vulnerable. Speak your self-love as passionately as you can. Share what you are going through from a perspective of loving yourself. Give yourself permission to laugh, cry, shake, or anything else to release any emotions you are experiencing.

*When you are the one listening.* Totally absorb your attention on the other person. Listen with your full energy, with your eyes, and with your body. Maintain eye contact. Be fully and totally present on a heart-centered level. Don't interrupt, offer advice, or step across their emotional boundaries. Their own healing intelligence is doing the work.

*Breathe the energy of love together.* You can also each place one hand on your heart and the other hand on your belly and do your own individual love-breathing work in the presence of each other.

*Do the affirmations and 12 steps.* You can also each tap your heart-centers with an open hand as you breathe deeply and repeat any of the affirmations, declarations, or statements contained in the 12 steps. You can also do step five with and for each other.

*Sexual and emotional boundaries if needed.* Going in without a clear communication of these boundaries will cause all kinds of hang-ups and expectations that could ruin the connection. At the outset, set these boundaries and clearly communicate them to each other if you feel they are needed.

## Intimate Relationships

Doing this work with someone whom you are in a committed and romantic relationship with can be tricky. When we are in these relationships, we are often running headlong into our own subconscious patterns, beliefs, and traumas. There are also many subconscious and cultural contracts, obligations, stories, and expectations about how we "should" be with each other.

When we start to authentically love, value, respect, and honor ourselves, that may conflict with all this subconscious programming. Self-love, as practiced in this book, can disrupt unconscious patterns in relationships, which in turn can stir up drama.

There are no hard-and-fast rules about whether to do this work with your partner. It will make sense for some couples and not for others. Some couples will find that having a self-love partner outside the relationship will help their connection grow, while some will want to do this work together.

*Both clearly committed to unconditional self-love.* When both partners are committed to growing in unconditional self-love, then the energy of that love will grow and envelope each of them. The whole relationship will be an energetic container of genuine unconditional love. You can even write and craft a relationship mission statement and/or intention that encompasses the commitment to this practice.

*All the above suggestions apply.* If you do this with your intimate partner, then all the above suggestions apply. Meet regularly, share listening time, etc.

*Combining autonomy with community.* If you do this work with your partner, it is also a good idea to have time in which you do this work autonomously, and then other times when you meet to work together. Do your best to strike a good balance between an *autonomy of practice* and a *community of practice*.

*Just one person doing this work.* If you are in a relationship and you are the only one doing this type of deep energetic self-love work, then your relationship could reach a point of being unsustainable. Perhaps not. It all depends on the individuals. Your work could help your partner shift toward self-love or push them away from it. It depends on them. All you can do is just keep doing your own work. Be patient and allow them time to come around. They either will or they won't.

One of the biggest messages of self-love we can send ourselves is that we are worthy of true love and lasting joyous connections. Connecting in relationships and partnerships with others who are doing this work can bring this point home to our hearts.

Danny Skyfeather

# The Mind-Chest Tapping Protocol

Danny Skyfeather

This protocol involves using your hand and fingertips to tap on specific acupressure points and energy centers. The intention is to create an energetic connection between them, and between your heart-center and spiritual eye. It helps foster heart-brain coherence. More specifically, you can use this method to install any of the commands of self-love directly into your nervous system and subconscious mind. You can use it while proceeding through the 90 days of additional affirmations and intentions. Of course, you can also use it with any other affirmations of your choosing. This protocol brings together principles found within energy psychology, energy healing, and hypnotherapy.

## The Mind-Chest Tapping Protocol

There are four tapping points with this protocol. They are intended to connect the mind with the chest and access the enormous healing power within you. Before you do the tapping protocol, it is always a good practice to take three super deep love-channeled breaths as you learned in practice #1. Then repeatedly tap each point from two to six seconds.

*(TFP) Triangle Forehead Point.* This point is a combination of the inside edge of each eyebrow and the elevated space between your eyebrows and the center of your forehead. To tap on this point, hold your index, middle, and ring fingers together. Begin tapping the space between your eyes and your forehead with all three fingers as a unit. If you use your right hand, the index finger lands on the inside end of your right eyebrow, the ring finger lands on the inside end of your left eyebrow, and the middle finger lands between your eyes but slightly elevated. If you use your left hand, the reverse applies. Depending on the dimensions of your own face, feel free to adjust your fingers slightly to have the tips of your fingers land on the above points. Also, see if you can tap *more* with the *fingerprint* area of your fingers and *less* with your *fingertips*. In this way, you are covering more surface area with each tap.

This point is triangular. Each eyebrow point and the space in the middle of your forehead, together, form this triangle.

When you tap with your three fingers as one unit, you are tapping on this entire space. Tapping on this point activates your prefrontal cortex and accesses your energetic "third eye." This is the seat of inner knowing, spiritual sight, visualization, and awakening. Tapping on this point before, during, or after any type of meditation or energy work will greatly enhance it.

(CP) *Chin Point*. This point is above your chin and below your bottom lip, right in the very middle. To tap on this point, hold your index and middle fingers together as a unit and begin tapping.

(DCP) *Double Collarbone Point*. The collarbone points are located slightly below the inside end of each collarbone, under the throat box and above the center of your chest. If you feel around this area you will find these points to be slightly tender if you press in on them. The practice is to tap on both at the same time. To do this, hold your thumb and middle/index fingers apart from each other as if you were grasping a small imaginary coffee mug. Then tap on both collarbone points at the same time. The tip of your thumb lands on one collarbone point and the tips of your middle and index fingers, as a unit, land on the other collarbone point.

(HCP) *Heart-Center Point*. This is the easiest of all the points. To tap on this point, simply tap the very center of your chest with an open hand just like you were tapping a drum. You can tap with all four fingers on the center of your chest, or with your whole hand.

The protocol is to start with the Triangle Forehead Point and move to the Chin Point, the Double Collarbone Point, and ending with the Heart-Center Point. Circle back up to the Triangle Forehead Point and start again. Each point should be repeatedly tapped for about two to six seconds. Always move swiftly from point to point.

When you do this you are creating a connection, or loop of energy, between your spiritual third eye, which is the center of *wisdom and understanding*, and your heart-center, which is the center of *feeling and devotion*. Both the spiritual eye and the heart-center are connected to the vibration of universal love that is present in all moments and times. Going from the spiritual eye to the chest and back again, repeatedly, opens the inner landscape of intelligence, energy, and information that is beyond your conscious awareness. This tapping procedure creates heart-mind coherence and harmony. You can use it to heal and transmute all sorts of deeply seated emotional issues within you.

Try this protocol now. As you do the following procedure, see if you can tap into the energetic connection with myself and everyone else doing this same thing. This protocol helps connect people across time and space. It opens your intuition. You can feel into what other people are going through. This helps you develop compassion and understanding in your relationships. Remember, each point should be firmly but gently tapped repeatedly for two to six seconds.

Taking three deep love-channeling breaths, let's go...

*Triangle Forehead Point...*
*Chin Point....*
*Double Collarbone Point...*
*Heart-Center Point...*

Immediately go back up to the Triangle Forehead Point and go through the protocol two more times. When you are finished, take three more love-channeled breaths. (3 breaths, 3 rounds, 3 breaths).

You can use this method as a stand-alone practice to help calm your emotions and balance the energy between your brain and heart. Practice often.

## Tapping the core heart-command

Now that you have learned this basic procedure, we can combine it with the repetition of our core command:

*I flood the energy of love through my mind and body*
*in all moments – and I open deeper to receive*
*and give this love to all life everywhere.*

Take three deep love-channeling breaths and begin the tapping protocol as you repeat the command out-loud with feeling and passion as follows:

(TFP) Triangle Forehead Point: *I flood the energy of love*
(CP) Chin Point: *through my mind and body in all moments*
(DC) Double Collarbone: *and I open deeper to receive and give*
(HC) Heart-Center Point: *this love to all life everywhere.*

Tap on each point for two seconds or more as you repeat each phrase of the command. Most importantly, hold the intention that you are literally tapping the command directly into your heart, nervous system, and subconscious mind. It is like you are downloading the program.

Once you have repeated the affirmation, circle back up to the Triangle Forehead Point and go through several more tapping/repetition rounds. When you are done with your mini-session, take three more deep love-channeling breaths to seal the process and reinforce the command within you. Your deep breaths work in harmony with the tapping.

Feel free to also time the tapping with the phrases of the command in any other way that you feel inclined to do so. Or you can simply tap and repeat without coordinating each phrase with each point. However, tapping the points in coordination with the four phrases of the command seems to work well. There are no rigid rules.

Speaking the command out-loud is really effective. This is because your voice is powerful. When you combine the breathing, the tapping, and speaking it out loud, you are fusing together your heart, voice, mind, and physiology. But again, there are no rigid rules. You can try speaking it silently, in a whisper, or out-loud.

## An optional post hypnotic suggestion

Toward the end of repeating the command and before you do your closing three deep breaths, you can repeat this affirmation while tapping on the points:

*I now activate the intention that my heart-center and subconscious mind will continue to repeat, feel, and actualize this heart-command in all the moments of my life to come.*

Repeat the core command one more time while tapping. Then take three breaths and end your session. In this way, you are sending a signal to your subconscious mind and heart-center to continue repeating the command in future moments, even if you are not consciously aware of it.

In hypnotherapy terms this is called a post-hypnotic suggestion. You could call your session of tapping a self-hypnosis session. You are taking deep breaths, tapping the points on your body while repeating the command, and then taking more deep breaths. This is creating a lot of moving parts for the conscious mind to pay attention to. The result is that the conscious mind gets distracted and the subconscious mind becomes more accessible. In this way you can create lasting change in your mind, habits, and energy levels.

You can also use Mind-Chest Tapping as mini self-love reboots throughout the day as follows...

### 3 breaths before and after

Just as described above, take three incredibly deep inhaling and exhaling breaths, tap all the points along the protocol three times, and then take three more deep breaths. Do this without focusing on any specific issue. This is a simple and super-fast tune-up.

There is a couple of points to remember about this. *One,* don't rush the breaths. Take three long deep breaths in and out of your nose, completely expanding and emptying your belly, chest, and lungs. *Two,* tap each point along the protocol for two to six seconds. *Three,* visualize and energetic thread swirling and connecting all the points. *Four,* do all of this while anchoring the energy and intention of unconditional self-love into your mind and body.

## 12-breath tapping reboot

You can also take extra time and do one deep breath per tapping point. Remember to 1) take your time with your breath, 2) tap each point for the entire time it takes to inhale and exhale, which is about 4 to 6 seconds, and 3) visualize the thread of energy connecting the points as you move one to the next, and 4) Flood the power and energy of unconditional love through your mind and body with each breath.

*12 breaths.* Repeatedly tap the Triangle Forehead Point while taking a very long and deep breath, in and out of your nose. Then immediately move to tapping the Chin Point while taking another long inhaling and exhaling breath. Proceed to tapping the Double Collarbone Point while taking another long breath. Then tap the Heart-Center Point while taking another one. Return to the top and start the process over. Go through all four points in this way, three times. When you are done you will have taken 12 deep breaths while tapping.

*Deep and long.* Be sure to keep your breaths very deep and long. Fill and empty your lungs completely. As you inhale, see and feel your belly and chest completely expand. As you exhale, allow both of them to completely deflate. Breathing through your nose is most beneficial. Nostril breathing filters the air and also helps activate your prefrontal cortex. However, you can try mouth breathing if you like. Doing deep and long breaths like this continuously does take a fair amount of practice.

*No pauses.* Allow no pauses between breaths and tapping. It is important to proceed directly to another tapping point and another breath when you have completed your exhale. This heightens your energetic vibration.

*Benefits.* The benefits of doing this are immense. As stated above, it helps build and grow the spiritual eye-heart-center connection. It blows the cobwebs out of your energetic system. It also helps you access your super-powers of creativity, intuition, insight, empathy, compassion, understanding, love, joy, gratitude, etc. It is also great to do as a re-boot when you are feeling stressed, as a break from a difficult conversation, when worried, or at any other time you just need to re-center yourself. It helps you internally let-go and rest in the essential state of your being.

*Eyes closed.* I would suggest closing your eyes and putting your phone or tablet away from you when doing your 12 breaths. Having your eyes closed helps create an inner restorative oasis within yourself. It signals that you are shutting out the distraction and noise of the world.

*Morning and evening.* The times right when you wake up and before sleep are great times to practice. Consider doing this as a routine before bed and in the morning. Another great time to do this is in the middle of the night when your mind is racing with thoughts and worries about the upcoming days or weeks. Just sit up in bed, do the tapping and breathing, and then lay back down. See if it can help calm your mind to sleep better.

*As a primer.* You can use the 12-breath tapping reboot before meditation, exercise, writing, painting, or any other activity that you want to have your energy balanced and harmonized for an optimal experience.

Danny Skyfeather

# 90-day Journey of
# Unconditional Self-Love

Danny Skyfeather

# 90-day Journey of Unconditional Self-Love

I am so honored and grateful that you have embarked upon this 90-day journey of unconditional self-love. What is so amazing is that the energy of love is everywhere present in all moments. On a silent and energetic level, we are walking together through every day of this journey. Although we do this work for ourselves, we are never alone.

When you breathe and heart-feel, vibrate, and resonate the Heart-Commands of Unconditional Self-Love within your chest and body, you are connecting with all beings doing the same thing. When you do the self-love breathing sessions, you are also silently connected with everyone else doing those very same sessions.

Remember that the love you give yourself will grow like beautiful flowers in the hearts and minds of those you love – and will also show up in the greater garden of all humanity. You are doing the earth a great service by loving yourself.

Each day come back to the four practices of 1) Breathing the energy of love through your mind and body in 20-minute sessions at a minimum... 2) Deep breathing and rapidly absorbing and reinforcing the Heart-Commands of Unconditional Self-Love... 3) Mirror work and 4) Self-care of your body, mind, and environment.

These four practices, combined together, will transform your life in extraordinary ways. Simple. Not always easy. But doable. If you miss a day, be kind to yourself. At your earliest opportunity, come back to the day you were at and continue. All prior gains are with you forever.

To get even more out of this experience, bathe your mind and body in 528 Hz music/sounds. Listen as often as you can. 528 Hz is considered to be the "miracle love frequency" and is believed to connect all hearts in the universe. Do a google search for 528 Hz or Solfeggio sounds, and you will find a plethora of artists to choose from.

On each of the upcoming days, there will be more short and potent commands and affirmations spoken from the *I am* perspective. Here are two great ways to work with them:

## Deep breathing and chest-tapping

Take three incredibly deep breaths, repeat the passage three times while tapping the center of your chest, and then take three more deep breaths. Feel as if you are tapping the words into your chest.

## Deep breathing and mind-chest tapping

This method is similar to the one above. Take three deep breaths, then repeat the passage three times while doing Mind-Chest Tapping, then close with three more deep breaths.

*"You, yourself, as much as anybody in the entire universe, deserve your love and affection."*
                    *Buddha.*

## Day 1

I am honored to begin and to deepen my journey of loving myself from a higher energetic perspective. With an expanding breath, I send waves of love to all future and past versions of myself along this journey. All futures and pasts are held in the light of love.

Going forward, I pledge to be kind and gentle with myself. Every day in every way, I will love myself more and more. With all my heart, power, and sincerity – I decide *now* to build an even stronger consciousness of genuine self-love within me.

## Day 2

I am willing to love myself with more sincerity and passion. In my simple willingness is found all the energy, power, motivation, tenacity, and persistence to keep going no matter what. May I always stay willing.

The essence of my very being is love. My core truth is love. I immerse myself in universal, joyous, and ever-new love. I bathe myself in the frequency and feeling of this love. I love myself with all the love in the entire universe.

## Day 3

I am worth the time it takes to build a mind and heart that is brimming over with self-love. I know that reconditioning my mind will take time and persistence. I deserve to love and value myself on deeper levels than before. I deserve to respect, care for, and speak well about myself in all moments. I deserve a life that reflects a healthy and radiant love for myself.

## Day 4

The love I give myself shows up as blossoming flowers in the hearts and minds of those I love. We are all connected on an inner level. Deep in our cells, and into our atoms and our energy, the line that seems to separate us blurs into a whirling mix of energy and information. The thoughts of love about myself that I hold as my feeling-truth will directly and positively impact those I love. I love myself to help nurture and create a self-loving and compassionate world.

## Day 5

I deserve my own limitless love. I deserve the sweet and nurturing presence and compassion of my infinite being. I feed myself emotionally from the delicious streams and rivers of love dancing through the sunlight of my imagination. Every day, I am open to more ways to cherish, care for, and nurture my entire being.

## Day 6

With each long and delicious breath IN – I open, expand, and raise my heart-center to the highest reaches of energy and consciousness. I merge in ecstatic oneness with all the love in the entire universe.

With each gentle and full breath OUT – I open the floodgates and pour all this love into my cells, heart, mind, emotions, and memories. All layers of my conscious, subconscious, and unconscious minds are bathed and held in this love. As I keep my breath flowing continuously – I relax and enjoy the feeling of this love pulsating through my entire being.

## Day 7

I trust that the energy of love is *intelligent* and is reaching the parts of me that words, language, and memory cannot reach. As I breathe deeply every day, flooding my body and mind with love, I realize that this energy is doing for me on a *primordial* and *subconscious* level what I am unable to do for myself on a *conscious* level. I am grateful for this flow of self-directed love.

## Day 8

My breath is my escape hatch into spirit. With each inhaling breath, the energy of my heart rises into omnipresent love. With each exhaling breath, all this love floods back into my human mind and body.

This energy is a sacred and continuous loop. When I am breathing in and up, the love is also flowing down and in. When the love is flowing down and in, the energy of my heart continues to also expand and rise. With all my heart, I feel into this continuous flow of love.

## Day 9

I bring the energy of my highest love to the corridors of my deepest fear. I allow the energetic wisdom of love to rain down upon the memories stored in my mind and body. All fear within me is wrapped in my own compassion, grace, understanding, and acceptance.

It's okay to be scared. I gently remind myself of this and love myself anyway. As I hold the frightened parts of me in the hands of love, I allow all fear within me to be cleared from my mind and body. I am so grateful.

## Day 10

I bathe my body and mind in pure joy. Joy cascades down through my mind and body in ever-increasing waves of light. I call to the most authentic joy of my soul to rise up from within the marrow of my bones. I am the joy that has never needed a reason to be, and I sink deeper into this exquisite truth.

## Day 11

I love, respect, and care for my physical body more and more. I am so grateful to bathe every cell of my body in waves of ever-increasing appreciation, love, and joy. I am a spiritual being of love that is living through this sacred body. In this spirit, I am grateful to care for my physical space, look after my health, eat good food, get plenty of rest, and move my body in ways that make me feel good. I deserve to feel good in every way imaginable.

## Day 12

I give my mind and body the space it needs to feel, to heal, and to grow. It is a privilege to feel and process all the painful, uncomfortable, and difficult emotions that may arise. I strive to completely accept myself for how I feel.

It is okay to feel whatever needs to be felt. I remind myself of this every day. As all emotions arise and pass through me, I allow myself to feel a little more alive. Self-acceptance is the law of my heart, mind, and body.

Danny Skyfeather

## Day 13

I am one-hundred-percent responsible to love myself unconditionally. I accept this responsibility. It is my job to parent myself, soothe my emotions, cheer myself onward, encourage and believe in myself, and to hold myself in the arms of grace and understanding when I make mistakes.

## Day 14

Doing this internal work will challenge and disrupt deep-seated unconscious patterns within me. These patterns are used to their routines and may stage internal rebellions. Emotional pain and dramas will arise.

When this happens, I commit to staying the course. I will feel what needs to be felt. I will keep breathing and keep channeling the highest love of the universe into and through my cells and atoms. I will keep tapping my chest and repeating these sacred commands of self-love. I will keep looking in the mirror and loving myself even more.

Danny Skyfeather

## Day 15

I make mistakes but I am not a mistake. I wrap arms of understanding around myself and allow myself to be human. Mistakes and blunders are the cracks through which the light of love can shine into this world. I am okay just as I am, even as I know I am improving with each step I take. Life is good and I am good. I am a precious and beautiful human being. I am perfectly imperfect.

## Day 16

There is beauty in the cracks of my heart. When the time is right, I allow the flood of tears to wash over me, to set my heartaches free, to heal my brokenness and loneliness, and to literally give my soul the wings to fly once again. Tears are the magical elixir from the heavens of my consciousness, telling me that it is okay to fall apart and to get up and dance one more time.

I give myself the sacred and eternal permission to crack open the caverns of my chest and allow all that is forgotten to flow into the sunlight of ever-increasing love.

## Day 17

It is my deliberate intention to drop my mind's awareness into the feeling kingdoms of my heart-center. This intention is activated with my deep and continuous breaths. With each long and delicious inhaling breath – I open the center of my chest wider. With each smooth and relaxing exhaling breath – I drop my mind into the soft and comforting space of my highest love. I keep breathing and allow my thoughts to drop into the wisdom of my chest.

My heart-center is the featherbed for my mind. It is a place to rest my thoughts and find solace in the embrace of my own love. My own soft and eternal love is my safe place to land.

## Day 18

Self-love is an ongoing process of growth. As I plunge my highest love into the furthest reaches of my unconscious mind and body, this love naturally causes old thoughts to come up to be released. *That's good.* As this process unfolds, I am bound to act in ways that do not reflect my commitment to love myself. *That's okay.* Thoughts of self-hatred and self-loathing can arise with a vengeance to knock me off the path of self-love. *All of this is okay.*

If I get down on myself for having thoughts of self-hatred, then these thoughts get bigger and stronger. The truth is that these thoughts are not who I am. They simply represent my old conditioning. It is my honor, privilege, and responsibility to witness these thoughts from a place of compassion and understanding. I was taught to hate myself, and I am now teaching myself to love my whole mind and body with ever-increasing gentleness.

Danny Skyfeather

## *Day 19*

I am lovable just as I am right now. I take several long and slow breaths and repeat this thought again. As I do, I send a gentle call to all the frozen parts of me that feel unlovable: *You are okay just as you are. You are included in the kingdom of my heart. There is nothing wrong with you.*

Through my continued passion and commitment to love myself on all levels of my mind and body – I give these lonely parts of me permission and freedom to step a little closer to the light of my heart.

Feeling unlovable is merely old conditioning that is being gently and patiently reconditioned over time. Every day in every way, deeper and deeper, I love the parts of me that feel unlovable. I accept myself wholly and unconditionally.

## Day 20

Doing this energetic and heart-based work of cultivating a consciousness of self-love can cause painful memories to arise. These memories are not in the past. They live in my body, right here and now. When these memories arise, I can step into the memory and repeat the core command of unconditional self-love. I become another character in the mental movie-house of the memory. I rhythmically and gently tap the center of my chest with an open hand as I keep repeating and feeling:

*I flood the energy of love through my mind and body*
*in all moments – and I open deeper to receive*
*and give this love to all life everywhere.*

Doing this alters the feeling and frequency of the emotional charge surrounding the memory. It helps all frozen parts of me to integrate into the spiritual light of my highest love expressed in this present moment.

## Day 21

I am committed to face and feel everything that arises from within me. In doing this, I begin from a state of gratitude. I am grateful for my breath and for each new moment that I get to live, love myself, and to grow.

From within this container of gratitude, I feel my emotions as I simultaneously relax and let-go. I allow the feelings to burn quickly and brightly through me, without gorging upon them and becoming a *pain alcoholic*. Gratitude shortens the lifespan of painful emotions and elongates the lifespan of joyous ones.

## Day 22

Loving myself is my sovereign right. Regardless of what other people think, say, or do – I still love, honor, and value myself. We are all connected on a cellular and subconscious level. When I begin to sincerely and passionately love myself, this can disrupt unconscious and unhealthy patterns in my relationships with other people.

When this happens, I am free to communicate what is in my heart. I will do my best to navigate to a higher level of functioning and connection in my relationships. Most of all, I am free to love myself no matter what. Self-love is the natural law that reigns supreme in all my relationships.

Danny Skyfeather

## Day 23

All my relationships are extensions of my fundamental relationship with myself. How I treat me is how I treat others. How I allow others to treat me is how I treat myself. Everything in my life reflects my relationship with myself.

Here and now, I deepen my sincere vow to treat myself with kindness, compassion, understanding, acceptance, and love. As I build this beautiful connection with myself, I will naturally see all my relationships improve for the better. I also realize that this process takes time. It is my ongoing intention to be patient with myself along the way.

## Day 24

I deserve, demand, and experience loving relationships. I set and anchor the intention into my heart-field that all my relationships are spiritual containers of unconditional love. I love myself with a fierce generosity of heart and allow this love to naturally extend to all the people I am in relationships with. In the embrace of unconditional love, I keep reminding myself that it is safe to love and be loved in return. I trust the energy of love.

Danny Skyfeather

## Day 25

Love wraps, dissolves, and consumes all material in its path, not out of war, but from a continuous inpouring of compassion. All the stuff in my body and mind – the cellular memories, old beliefs, stored traumas, disempowering stories – anything that does not reflect my highest joy – is dissolved and consumed by the fire of my growing self-love.

Everything that appears to be contrary to love becomes fuel for my growth. The core of love that I am does not defend and therefore can never attack. Love disarms through the power of its innocence.

## *Day 26*

My circular breath is a transmission device, carrying the highest love of my soul into the depths of my mind and body, and back again. I breathe my heart into the universe and cascade love into my body and mind now. Like a waterfall that never ends, I shower myself in pure spiritual light. As I keep my breathing rhythm continuous and unbroken, I tap into the magnificent joy of being alive.

Danny Skyfeather

## Day 27

There were times in my childhood where my physical and emotional needs were not met. I deserved to have been fully cared for. However, it is now my responsibility to care for myself. I accept this responsibility with a full and open heart.

The energy of love is everywhere present in all moments of time. With the power of my intentional imagination – I see this love locating all these moments of my past where I didn't get what I needed. I wrap all of them in genuine acceptance, compassion, and understanding.

## Day 28

I gently allow my heart-center to be open, closed, or slightly cracked. With a soft approach, I ask the core of my fragile heart if it's ready to open a little more. Then I accept, honor, and appreciate all that I hear.

There is no prying the inner doors open. My vulnerable heart deserves to be cared for and protected. It has its own wisdom and timing in which to open. I am grateful to be a fierce and gentle warrior of love for the core of sweetness and innocence within me.

Danny Skyfeather

## Day 29

I send waves of unconditional love cascading through my skull, face, and eyes. My arms, legs, muscles, tissues and cells are all bathing in the highest frequency of this love. All fear, shame, and regrets within me are located, held, and healed in this love. All the seeds of joy, bliss, and delight within me are watered and nurtured into growth by this love.

## Day 30

I love myself by getting moving, even if I don't want to. Washing the dishes. Cleaning the house. Exercising. Doing what needs to be done. These are all exercises in self-love. Self-discipline – when applied with gentleness, grace and joy – is self-love.

## Day 31

I am committed to cultivating positive, encouraging, and uplifting self-talk. I believe in myself and in the power of my dreams. I have everything it takes to shine my brilliance into the world. I am worth it. I am okay just as I am. I am perfect, whole, and complete. I deserve to experience the full cascade of abundance and joy in all areas of my life. It's up to me to talk to myself in empowered and uplifting ways. It's my job to love myself when nobody is looking.

## Day 32

I fiercely guard my dreams and goals. I don't let any relationship take me away from their loving pursuit. If I do, then I hold myself responsible and not the relationship.

It is so easy to put the dreams, needs and desires of someone else ahead of my own. I will not bury my joy to please others anymore. The truth is that my joy has value. My dreams are worth my time and effort. I am one-hundred-percent responsible to follow through and fulfill them. It is nobody else's job but my own to believe in myself. My dreams and my joy are equally as valuable to me as the success of my relationships.

Danny Skyfeather

# Day 33

*Healing anxiety.* To clear anxiety and fear from my body and mind, I take three love-channeling breaths and repeat this statement three times with passionate feeling (as I either tap the center of my chest, or tap the points of the Mind-Chest Tapping Protocol)...

*Even though I feel scared and anxious – I love, honor, and accept myself anyway. I give myself permission to feel this fear from a place of genuine acceptance. I accept myself for exactly how I feel. Even as I feel afraid, I activate the intention that the energy of love now locates, heals, and releases the roots of this fear. In all the moments of my life to come, whether a day, a week, or even years from now – my deeper intelligence will continue to locate, heal, and release the roots of fear and anxiety in my body and mind. This process will continue within, below, and beyond my conscious awareness.*

I take three more deep breaths and relax.

## Day 34

The thoughts of self-love that I willfully and passionately plant into my chest, body, and subconscious mind will silently produce still more thoughts of a like nature on their own. With persistent practice, self-love becomes automatic, joyous, and spontaneous. It becomes a new program running in the background of my consciousness.

For too long, the old conditioned programs of self-hatred and shame have run my mind and body. I intentionally change the laws of my subconscious mind to self-love, self-joy, self-compassion, self-appreciation, and self-acceptance. In each new moment of my life to come, I will continue to renew and reinforce this new internal reality.

## *Day 35*

I am honored and grateful to be me. I love and appreciate my personality. I am grateful for all my unique quirks. It is an honor and a privilege to be alive and breathing. I am grateful for my breath as it flows smoothly in and out of my lungs and body. I am grateful for the many ways that I shine my light into the world.

## Day 36

I will stop expecting other people to love me, for me. When I delegate the responsibility to love myself to others, then it becomes a messy bog. The hole in me gets deeper and I try to put other people in a bondage that they cannot escape. They always end up being human. They fail to love me in the way I think they should. The truth is that it was never their job to begin with. Loving myself has always been my job.

I am turning this around. I am committed to loving myself passionately and unconditionally. From this foundation, other people can join the party, but they don't have to. I have it covered. The love I give myself is more than enough to meet my emotional needs. This frees other people and myself.

Danny Skyfeather

## Day 37

The love I give myself grows in the hearts of those I relate to, and also reaches the collective heart and mind of all humanity. We are all connected on an inner level. I am doing a great service to the planet when I place my hand on my heart and love myself with sincere joy. A loving world begins when individuals make the internal shift into a healthy state of self-love. I do my part by loving myself a little more each day.

## Day 38

My external space reflects my internal state. All I need to do is look around me to see how I feel about myself. If my physical environment is in chaos, then I know there is work I need to do. This is not a time to berate myself. Instead, it is a golden chance to understand, accept, and love myself. Slowly but surely, my physical environment will naturally begin to reflect my growing state of internal self-awakening and love. I love myself by taking good and loving care of the physical space that I live in.

Danny Skyfeather

## Day 39

The voice in my head that judges other people or myself is rooted in emotional pain of some kind. When thoughts of criticism and judgment arise, this is my opportunity to direct the energy of love into the roots of that emotional pain. *I just send the love and let love do its thing.* Love will then travel to the root cause of this judging voice and wrap it in gentle compassion and understanding.

I unconditionally love the voice in my head that criticizes and judges myself and others. As I do, I allow this voice to unfold and reveal to me the pain that it is holding. As this pain is revealed, I sink even deeper into self-acceptance and love.

## Day 40

I bathe all my unconscious cellular memories in the light of ever-new love and joy. My body carries the memories of my past, and it is my solemn honor to release and forgive all these memories. I place my hands of light upon any part of my body and say with feeling and heightened internal intensity: *I love you, thank you, forgive you, and release you.*

I repeat these statements over and over again as I intend that they are spoken through my hands and communicated into my cellular memories. I breathe deeply and allow the currents of my breath to carry them into the furthest reaches of my cells.

I allow the powers of gratitude, forgiveness, and love to reach into the tiny caverns and alleyways of memory that my body holds. I see all these memories being released.

## Day 41

I strive to eat clear, clean food that is brimming with life-force energy. I ingest foods that I first saturate with love. As I prepare food, I think thoughts of love toward myself and others. When I consume this food, I am taking in the thoughts that I held in my mind as I prepared it.

My relationship with food is my relationship with myself. I love myself by eating good and nutritious food. At the same time, when I eat food that is less than healthy, I am kind and gentle with myself. Emotionally beating myself up for eating "bad" food only increases the desire for that kind of food. Instead, I wrap my arms of compassion around the part of me that wants to eat food that is less than healthy.

In my quest to eat healthier food, I love and accept myself always. In being present and gentle with myself, my health naturally improves. I deserve to live in a body that overflows with health, vitality, and joy.

## Day 42

There are times in my life when saying no to myself, and to what I may want in the moment, is a way to nurture my long term emotional and physical health. It is okay to say no to temporary pleasures for the sake of longer-term growth. It is my job to be the parent of my impulses, saying no when appropriate and yes when it is right.

## Day 43

Self-gentleness is the key to self-love. When I falter, make mistakes, fall or jump off the self-love train, eat junk food, get depressed, lash out, act out, or behave in any way that is less than loving – all these are great opportunities to wrap myself in a gentle hug. I can say to myself: *It's okay. You're okay. You're only human. You're still a good person. I still love you. It's going to be okay, etc.* It is my job to self-soothe. It is up to me to mother myself when I make a mistake.

## Day 44

Loving myself in this profound way – both with the spoken words of love and with the unspoken energy of love – is not always easy. Sometimes it is extremely hard. Pain comes up, emotions feel raw, and life feels hard. It is in these times that I choose to dig underneath the pain and just keep going.

Planting my bare feet on the earth and taking deep breaths. Talking to someone. Getting support. Taking a bath. Taking a walk. These are a few of the things I can do to get through the rough emotional times.

The truth is that there is gold underneath every painful emotion. I deserve to find this gold. So if there is stuff coming up, this is a good sign that this process is working. I love myself by moving forward. I deserve the long-term benefits that come from practicing self-love in the emotional trenches of life.

## Day 45

There are many younger versions of myself living inside my body and mind. With an expanding breath, I send a pulse of love to them all. I send the highest vibration of love to all the ordinary, painful, and joyous moments of my past. I whisper messages of hope into the ears of all my past selves who feel alone, lost, scared, and in pain: *You will make it. You will. I promise. I believe in you. You have more strength, love, and courage inside you than you realize. Keep going no matter what. I love you.* I send these messages of love and trust that they find their way to the hearts of my younger selves.

## Day 46

From a higher spiritual perspective – I flood my mind and body with love. I wrap my unconscious shadows in the energy of forgiveness. In the name of love, I forgive myself on the subatomic levels of my being.

Love is intelligent energy that travels through the depths of my psyche to heal and release that which is beyond the reach of my thinking mind. I trust in the flow of this love and hold the intention that the miracle of forgiveness is silently growing within the unconscious depths of my being.

## Day 47

The whole exists within each part of the whole. I am a part that contains the whole, and I am so grateful to feel and enjoy this truth. As I love myself, I love the whole universe that dwells within me. I am a Child of the Infinite. I relax, smile, and rest in the awe and sheer beauty of this truth.

## Day 48

I love others as myself and I love myself in others. As I extend compassion to others, I am loving myself. I am within other people and other people are within me. We are wrapped up inside each other, even as we appear to be separate. To love myself is the very definition of loving others. To love and serve others is to love and serve my very own soul.

## Day 49

I now stop taking crap from the voices in my head that tell me that I am less than magnificent. I tap my chest, or pound my chest if need be, and literally command that these old lies and conditioning leave my body now. It is time to step up. No more excuses. With all the joy and power of my soul – I declare that unconditional love is the supreme law of my body and mind.

## Day 50

I love myself in the presence of other people that I love and trust. It is one thing to love myself while sitting alone, and quite another thing to love myself in the presence of others. It takes tremendous courage and vulnerability to love myself with other people watching.

I will do what it takes to cultivate and practice self-love in front of others. At the same time, I fiercely guard my heart from those who are not safe, and who have not earned the privilege to see inside me.

Danny Skyfeather

## Day 51

I gently hold myself as an infant child and wrap my baby self in love. With my creative imagination, I step back in time and walk up to the crib where I am sleeping as an infant child. I gaze in awe and wonder at the miracle of my own birth. With gentle arms, I pick myself up and hold myself. Breathing deeply, I wrap my baby self in all the light, all the joy, and all the love in the entire universe. I give myself all the love I needed, wanted, and desired. I feel all this love pouring through my heart and hands – gently enfolding my infant self.

In my mind's eye, I step back and see a vision of my adult self holding my baby self. I wrap that scene in even more love, and see it permanently anchored in my chest and body. In all the moments of my life to come, I will continue to hold my baby self in gentleness, peace and love.

## Day 52

With all the power of my deliberate intention, I smile with the light in the center of my chest. I turn this smile back inward upon myself. I smile into my heart, into my mind, and into my soul. As I do, every cell and atom of my body and mind lights up.

## Day 53

With every long inhaling breath – my heart expands and rises into a higher state of love. With every smooth exhaling breath, all this love floods back into and through my mind and body. As I keep breathing, this energy keeps flowing. It is an unbroken circle of energy.

This love knows exactly what inside me needs healing and attention. I trust this process. There is nothing more I need to know or do, but to simply enjoy the feeling of energetic love coursing through my veins and bursting with joyous abandon through my wide-open heart.

## Day 54

With passionate intensity – I repeat and feel this command from the center of feeling in my chest, 3 times in a row: *Immersed in the infinite love that I am – I love myself wholly and unconditionally.*

This statement affirms that my home is in a place of love that transcends time and space – and from this higher place – I love all levels of my body and mind. I love all the moments of my life with fierce and gentle tenacity.

I coordinate this thought with my breath. Breathing in... *Immersed in the infinite love that I am* ... breathing out... *I love myself wholly and unconditionally.*

I keep breathing and repeating this command for as long as I like. As I drop this thought onto the currents of my breath – it is carried into the subatomic depths of my being.

Danny Skyfeather

## Day 55

As my self-love increases, my selfishness decreases. This is because, when I am feeling more selfish, I am demanding that my needs get met from the outside. I am thinking about what I am getting and not getting from others. This is a downward spiral.

On the other hand, when I am in self-love, all my emotional needs are already being met by myself, so there is a lesser need to seek validation outside of me. This frees me to think of other people more, and to be of better service. This is an upward spiral.

## Day 56

If I love myself, then the whole world could be against me, and I would be okay. If I hate myself, then the whole world could line up and tell me how loved I am, and I wouldn't believe a single word anyone says. It is my commitment to love myself as sincerely as possible. My genuine love for myself opens inner doors to receive even more love from others.

## Day 57

My own heart is the direct route to other hearts. The surest way for my love to reach others is to send it cascading into myself. Loving myself is loving others because we are all entangled on a deep energetic level.

All life is within. When I breathe the energy of my highest love into my body, mind, and emotions – I am directly loving all of life. When I send love to others, I am receiving that love myself. All that I give is given to me.

## Day 58

It is my intention to transform the conditioned patterns of self-hatred within me into blossoming flowers of self-love. I do this by the consistent and persistent application of compassion toward myself.

I look honestly and gently at any entrenched self-loathing that might still be lingering within me. When I see these old thoughts, beliefs, feelings, and patterns coming to the surface – I respond with a hand on my heart and a deliberate breath of understanding and love.

Danny Skyfeather

## Day 59

I give my body the energy of unconditional peace. Peace to my *belly*, *heart*, *body*, and *mind*. I see my belly being filled to overflowing with the energy of liquid peace. I see this peace rising up and overflowing my heart. Then every cell of my body gets to feel this peace. As my belly, heart, and body are bathed in peace – my mind and thoughts are filled with peace as well. Every day in every way, I give myself permission to feel even more peace.

## *Day 60*

Self-love requires cultivation, patience, and practice. I honor and appreciate myself for all the inner work I have done and all that I will do. I am worth the time it takes to build a fortress of self-awakening, love, and joy within all levels of my heart and mind. I will keep moving forward no matter what.

## Day 61

I give myself the gift of free and flowing laughter every day. Laughter is itself a reason to laugh. As I laugh with myself and others, I am more able to feel the energy of love reach deeper into my body and mind.

I love myself by dropping the curtain of seriousness from my awareness. I let-go of taking myself or life too seriously. I was born to experience joy, laughter, lightness, happiness, freedom, and bliss. In giving myself permission to feel good, I rise to new levels of self-appreciation, love, and joy.

## Day 62

I believe in myself with all my heart, mind, and soul. If I do not believe in myself, then nobody else will. I believe in my own beauty, worth, and abilities. I believe in my own dreams and visions. It is up to me and nobody else. Every day in every way, my belief in myself grows stronger. I have faith in my own brilliance.

Danny Skyfeather

## Day 63

Thoughts that are firmly planted in my heart will populate my mind. I now take several deep and delicious breaths. With all my passionate intensity, I tap the center of my chest with an open hand and repeat, feel, and vibrate these commands of self-love:

*I love myself with the energy of ever-new joy.*
*Pure liquid joy courses through my veins.*
*I bathe my cells in my highest joy.*

I repeat these statements as many times as my heart desires. I see and visualize that the words themselves, and their essence, are anchored inside my body.

## Day 64

I love and hold my inner child in arms of light. I am a warrior of peace, healing, and compassion for my beautiful and creative inner child. Love reaches into all my memories as I bring the past into this present moment. Love is here and now. I cherish, adore, and protect the beautiful and immortal innocence of my inner child.

Danny Skyfeather

## Day 65

Every day in every way, I am even more relaxed, calm, and grateful. I give myself plenty of time to completely relax every cell, muscle, and tissue of my body. I see how relaxed I can allow myself to be.

I love myself by giving myself breaks where I can totally relax. A nap. Five minutes of relaxing every cell of my body. A barefoot walk in the park. Laying under a tree and watching the branches sway in the wind. It is during these times that I cultivate a calm and balanced state of being. Relaxation is self-love.

## Day 66

With a long and intentional breath, I see and feel my voice and my throat expanding and opening. I love what I have to express, and I deserve to be heard and understood. I will no longer suppress my voice to appease other people.

Honoring my voice is a process and a journey, and I will be gentle with myself along the way. Regardless of what other people think, I value what I have to say. I value my life experience and the beautiful ways that I express myself.

Danny Skyfeather

## Day 67

The thoughts that I deliberately think as I am falling asleep are the very same thoughts I wake up to. The quality of my day begins the night before. As I fall asleep, I deeply think thoughts of love, appreciation, and joy toward myself. I intend that these thoughts will be carried into my dreamtime to sprout and grow in the soft light of the morning.

## Day 68

I have the power to choose my thoughts. With a deep breath, I concentrate my awareness into the front part of my mind. What thoughts of self-love do I choose to think today? What thoughts will I drop down into the feeling centers of my chest? What thoughts will I dwell upon?

I create my life according to the thoughts and beliefs toward myself that I hold in my mind and heart. I practice thinking and feeling thoughts of love, esteem, appreciation, and belief toward myself. From the foundation of these thoughts, my whole life is created anew.

Danny Skyfeather

## Day 69

I rest my hands upon my body, breathe continuously, and pour the energy of unconditional joy into my cells and atoms. My hands are emissaries of divine joy – giving this energy to all the layers of my mind and body. I deserve to experience joy for no reason.

## Day 70

I emotionally move into joy, even if doing so risks the destruction of all that is familiar and comfortable. At first, I may get frightened by the feeling of this joy. This is okay. I love myself through the fear and keep going anyway.

Living my joy requires the courage to be vulnerable. As I embrace my vulnerability, I let-go and allow myself to be carried to my greatest joy.

*Love is joy – joy is love – I am love – I am joy.*

Danny Skyfeather

## Day 71

It is my sacred intention that my inner and growing love for myself be spontaneous, natural, and organic. May loving myself be as natural and easy for me as breathing. In the hours, days, weeks, and years to come – I joyously expect that feelings of love, respect, gratitude, and compassion toward myself will effortlessly rise and express themselves within me.

## Day 72

Yes. I deserve all the joy, love, and abundance in the entire universe. I certainly do. It is okay for me to be happy and to feel at ease. I am glad to be joyous, free, and connected. I will not always feel good. That's okay too. But when the good feelings come knocking on the door of my heart, I will not shrink away from them. Yes is a beautiful affirmation when it comes to feeling good and happy about myself.

Danny Skyfeather

# Day 73

I forgive and release my ancestors. I release myself from all unconscious contracts that may have been passed down to me. I do not have to live out and perform the unspoken obligations of my ancestors. I am my own unique sovereign being with a spiritual calling to chart my own path. I let-go of the cellular and subconscious bonds with my ancestors that no longer serve my highest emotional and spiritual growth. I place my loving hands on my heart, take several deep and continuous breaths, and repeat these statements multiple times with emotional intensity:

To my mom and all ancestors before her, I declare with all my heart, mind, and soul: *I love you, thank you, forgive you, and release you.*

To my dad and all ancestors before him, I declare with all my heart, mind, and soul: *I love you, thank you, forgive you, and release you.*

I send this energetic program down into my cells and atoms. It is my deliberate intention that all unhealthy cords of shame, guilt, obligation, and codependency with my ancestors be released from all levels of my mind and body. It is my further intention that all healthy bonds with my ancestors continue to thrive and grow within me.

## Day 74

I dedicate the love I give myself to the immediate benefit of all life on this planet. In a paradoxical way, loving myself is not all about me. Yes, I am involved. I value and honor myself. I give myself all the compassion, presence, and understanding that I need. Yet, the energy of love is a continuous flowing stream. Love can never be held or contained. It can only flow.

I shower myself in love – then relax and allow this energy to inwardly rush to all life everywhere. All life benefits from the love I give myself.

Danny Skyfeather

## Day 75

What happened to me as a child was never my fault, but it is my *one-hundred-percent-now-responsibility* to hold and heal myself. I love every old wound, trauma, and hurt within me. I hug myself with my gentle arms of immortal joy. None of it was ever my fault, and I forgive the small sweet part of me that took the blame. It's okay. I send the highest compassion of my soul to this part and say: *I love you. It was never your fault. You are okay. You are safe now. There is nothing wrong with you.*

Every layer of memory in my body and mind is held in the light of my heart and soul. In this love, I declare that I am not broken. There wasn't anything wrong with me then and there is nothing wrong with me now. I am perfect, whole, and complete just as I am.

## Day 76

There is no such thing as character defects, only parts of my being that are crying out for love and attention. As I give these parts the energy and compassion they deserve, they are healed from within. Every single part of me deserves the full magnificence of my love.

Danny Skyfeather

## Day 77

There is loving myself unconditionally, and then there is unconditionally receiving this love. Receiving my own love can be an emotional challenge at times, but it is doable.

I am committed to cultivating the trust required to receive my own love. This trust requires vulnerability. With the powers of trust and vulnerability – I am growing in my inner ability to receive my own love.

## Day 78

I am worthy of true love and genuine connection. When shame arises that tells me otherwise, I step back and name it. Shame ceases to have power over me once it is brought into the light of awareness.

I don't have to suppress my shame under a smile and pretend that I am feeling okay when I am not. If I am feeling any shame at all, this is my opportunity to love the part of me that feels this way. It's okay. I accept, honor, and love myself for however I am feeling in this moment. Further, I get to talk about it with someone I love and trust. No more shall shame or fear rob my opportunities for love and connection.

Danny Skyfeather

## Day 79

I embrace whatever I am feeling. I no longer need to numb out and seek ways to get out of my body. The truth is that it is safe to fully be in my body. I will say this again with even more feeling: *It is safe to fully be in my body.*

As I repeat this statement, I place my hand on my chest and send the energy of compassion to the part of me that doesn't feel safe. It's okay to feel unsafe, and I know that this feeling can be gently changed and transformed. *It is safe to fully be in my body.*

## Day 80

With understanding and acceptance – I acknowledge that there are times when it's hard to connect with my emotions. That's okay. I simply breathe my heart open wider and send love to the part of my mind that disconnects from what I am feeling.

Perhaps there were times in my life as a child when my small body and mind just couldn't handle the magnitude of what I was going through. In response, my mind dissociated from those experiences. This is a survival mechanism that I am grateful for. At the same time, I remind myself that I am now safe to feel all my emotions. *I was not safe then, but I am safe now.*

Danny Skyfeather

## Day 81

I look back and see that there were times in my past where my physical, emotional, and mental boundaries were crossed and there was nothing I could do about it. Perhaps I was a child and powerless to stop it. Even as an adult, there have been times where I let my boundaries be crossed. I forgive the past completely. I forgive it all.

Right now, I have the power to set clear, healthy, and loving boundaries with people. Not everyone is welcome in my personal, emotional, mental, and spiritual space. My job is to set the boundary. How other people react to that boundary is on them. I am a loyal warrior of peace and protection for myself. I love myself by setting boundaries and enforcing them.

## Day 82

I love myself by asking for help when I need it. I am on this journey with other people, and I deserve to get help as I need it. I am free to ask for a listening ear, to get support, give and receive a hug, etc. I am free to sit under a tree with my bare feet on the soil and ask for help from the Earth, Sky, and Universe. Help is always available to me.

Danny Skyfeather

## Day 83

I love myself by putting in the work. Even when I don't feel like doing what needs to be done, I muster the inner resolve and do it anyway. I believe in the power and magic of my dreams. I deserve happiness and fulfillment, so I put in the work. I am grateful for all that I have done so far, and I am grateful for all that I will do tomorrow.

## Day 84

With the power of my brilliant imagination, I visualize that my body and mind is held within an unbroken circle and container of unconditional love. This circle enfolds my entire body, the space around my body, and all layers of my mind.

With each deliberate breath, I raise my heart-field into the highest reaches of my soul and continuously cascade love into this circle now. Throughout the day, I am so grateful to take a few breaths, visualize this circle, and feel this love flooding through it.

Danny Skyfeather

## Day 85

The highest vibration of love is now infused into my deepest human experience. I love myself as a child, as an adolescent, as a young adult, as a mature adult, and as an elderly adult. I love myself in the very moment of my birth, my death, and everything in between. I love all moments of my life – whether mundane, extraordinary, painful, sleeping, waking, dreaming, loving, or working. I love it all with the fierce generosity of my soul.

## Day 86

I radically forgive everything within me. With the power of my inner sword of pure forgiveness, I break the river of toxic shame flowing through my bloodline. The sickness stops here.

Down into the basement of my unconscious mind, I forgive myself. Fear and shame shall not pass into this present moment. Through *energetic forgiveness*, I manifest the power of love in my life.

## Day 87

I respect myself. This self-respect grows clearer every day. It shines through my eyes and is reflected back to me in my physical environment. It is clearly communicated to others through my words and actions.

I respect the beautiful soul that I am. From the foundation of this respect, I deserve to experience all the good that life has to offer. I deserve all the happiness, joy, love, and abundance that I could possibly experience, and more. I love myself by respecting my body, by respecting my mind, and by respecting the awe-inspiring miracle of being alive.

## Day 88

I declare with all my heart, soul, and strength that self-love is the very law of my mind, body, relationships, and life. Every day from this day forward, I will continue to honor, appreciate, love, and respect myself even more.

Danny Skyfeather

## Day 89

I look into the windows of my own eyes and behold the magnificent being that I am. I cherish and adore the miracle of my existence. I appreciate being alive. I eat foods that nourish and support my wholeness, radiant health, and vitality. I move my body and exercise in ways that support my joy, connection, and happiness. I care for my physical environment.

Most of all, I practice self-love with constant repetition. *I work at it.* I am worth the time it takes to build a mind, body, and life that reflects my highest self-love and respect.

I will never give up. Every time I fall, get sidetracked or distracted, I will get back up again. Regardless of how long I stay down, I will be courageous and gentle with myself and rise again.

## Day 90

This is just the beginning. As I continue this journey of loving myself in the most sincere and healthy ways possible, may I always have the mind and heart of a beginner.

Self-love is a process and not a destination. It is a journey. Each step is a new beginning. Each morning, may I wake up with thoughts of appreciation, joy, and gratitude toward myself. May I fall asleep in a blanket of loving self-directed thoughts.

May this energy of self-love extend inwardly and silently to all beings in the universe. May the energy of love that I give myself benefit all life in the most joyous ways possible. May this love also reach into the very core of reality – touching the heart of the universe and returning to me in torrential downpours of joy.

Danny Skyfeather

## Onward

Awesome!

You did it!

You are amazing in every way!

Now that your journey is complete, do your best to keep going. Consider starting again. Although you do this work alone, you are not alone. I am here if you need support. Reach out anytime via email at: dannyskyfeather@gmail.com.

My website is: www.dannyskyfeather.com

*notes:*

Danny Skyfeather

*notes:*

*notes:*

Danny Skyfeather

Made in the USA
Las Vegas, NV
23 April 2022

47911117R00114